The Talent Revolution

"The world is facing unprecedented existential challenges, some that threaten all we know. What's clear is that the thinking that got us here will not be the thinking that gets us to where we need to be—as organizations, communities, and individuals. We need to create a fresh environment where we can all flourish and thrive. To do that we need to change our understanding of how we unleash and harness the total potential of our people. The challenges we face are that huge. And that means starting a Talent Revolution. If you're not sure how to trigger that revolution, this book is a good place to start. Just remember the clock is ticking."

—DAVID PERRING

Director of Research, Fosway Group—Europe's #1 HR industry analyst

"I have known Anne for years and have seen first-hand her commitment to revolutionizing the talent experience. Her work and her fierce determination to improve businesses and the lives of the employees that work there are testaments to this. She knows it isn't easy but, in her book, she uses real case examples and her own experience working deeply with clients in need of transformation to draw a roadmap that makes it possible."

—MOLLIE LOMBARDI

Founder and Principal Analyst

T0273919

"Anne Fulton has fostered in many ways the Golden Age of HR Technology, where employees are at the center of all talent strategies. Her ability to focus on the interconnection between talent attraction, growth, career, culture, and AI is a master class on the future of employee experience."

—LARRY MCALISTER
Vice President of Global Talent, NetApp

"During COVID, Anne Fulton used her time wisely to write *The Talent Revolution*. She sagely explains why we need a completely new way of approaching talent mobility, why it's essential to employee engagement, experience, and retention, and why so many leaders eschew it. Fulton also describes how a free talent marketplace upends the traditional, hierarchical career ladder and gives employees a voice. Having coined the phrase 'The Great Escape' while millions quit their jobs, Fulton makes the case for employee flexibility in terms of work location and schedule flexibility. Ultimately, she asks executives, 'When it comes to your employees, what are you willing to fight for as we come to terms with the unstoppable sea changes from COVID?'"

—ROBIN ERICKSON, PhD
Vice President, The Conference Board

"Anne Fulton is a visionary for a democratized talent experience and, with Fuel50, has been the first to launch a talent marketplace to the world with FuelGigs in 2018. True visionaries for the future of work, Anne and the team at Fuel50 have not only championed a future of work vision, they have architected a solution that delivers real business value."

—JOSH BERSIN
President, Founder, and Author, The Josh Bersin Company

Talent
Revolution

THE
Talent
Revolution

ANNE FULTON

Optimizing our workforce for the new talent economy

Forbes | Books

Published by Forbes Books, Charleston, South Carolina.
Member of Advantage Media.

Forbes Books is a registered trademark, and the Forbes Books colophon is a trademark of Forbes Media, LLC.

Printed in the United States of America.

10 9 8 7 6 5 4 3 2 1

ISBN: 978-1-95588-479-2 (Paperback)
ISBN: 978-1-95588-480-8 (eBook)

LCCN: 2022920844

This custom publication is intended to provide accurate information and the opinions of the author in regard to the subject matter covered. It is sold with the understanding that the publisher, Forbes Books, is not engaged in rendering legal, financial, or professional services of any kind. If legal advice or other expert assistance is required, the reader is advised to seek the services of a competent professional.

Since 1917, Forbes has remained steadfast in its mission to serve as the defining voice of entrepreneurial capitalism. Forbes Books, launched in 2016 through a partnership with Advantage Media, furthers that aim by helping business and thought leaders bring their stories, passion, and knowledge to the forefront in custom books. Opinions expressed by Forbes Books authors are their own. To be considered for publication, please visit **books.Forbes.com**.

To my inspiring family. You bring joy to me and the fabulous Fuellies I have the privilege of working with around the world.

CONTENTS

ACKNOWLEDGEMENTS

Firstly thank you to Hannah Todd for your research and editing skills and encouragement to bring this book to life. You made a difference to this work. Special thanks go to a few Fuellies in particular, whose work, thought leadership, and expertise have played a huge role in this book—Emily Morris, John Hollon, and Marija Potter. Your work on our talent mobility research project, insights, expertise, and talent shine in this book, which deserves enormous credit to the work you have contributed to enhancing the talent experience across the globe. Thanks to Jo Mills, Amy Centers, Christine du Plessis, and the teams they lead, for their work in creating inspiring workplaces and change and transformation in every organization they touch. Your ideas and inspiration are infused in this work. Thank you to every Fuellie I work with around the world, who has educated me and inspired me with the work you all contribute to our mission of making a difference to the future of employees and the organizations they work in.

Now Is the Time for Revolution

The year 2020 was not normal.

One week into social isolation here in New Zealand, where I once lived, we were under military guard—two military guards for every one civilian inmate. This was a "life-lockdown," albeit a slightly more luxurious one than a prison camp in that I could order coffee between 9:00 and 11:00 a.m., and I was allowed 750 ml of wine per day.

On my first day of lockdown, I was arrested for going out for a run, even though I was the only person in the 20-by-20 exercise yard at the time, and I promised to leave as soon as another person showed up. That arrest is now on my police record; it was even escalated to the Ministry of Health, as I was put under the threat of being sanctioned simply for wanting to jog for the sake of my mental health.

On Day 4, I was cautioned for talking to a neighbor while doing our rounds, even though we were masked and at a respectable social distance.

On Day 5, my thinking started to shift. I started to reframe this as a rare opportunity in life for reflection and reframing. And after all, who can complain about being locked in a room for 14 days with only Netflix for company?

On Day 6, I started to write.

As Viktor Frankl noted, there is nothing like enforced captivity to deliver creativity.

All these limitations on my freedom made me think about the talent liberation that we need more urgently than ever in organizations across the globe—talent agility, talent empowerment, talent enablement, the true emancipation of our talent that we need to deliver to the increasingly challenging world we live in.

The traditional talent processes that put people into boxes served the purposes of the last decade, the last millennium even. But we have reached a point where we need to rethink how we engage with our people. Now is the era for a truly humanistic-existential approach to talent. What we need now is a talent revolution where we can all become equal citizens in a democratized world. Now is the time to be a talent revolutionary—a Karl Marx of the new talent experience.

The good news is there's never been such a time for disruption.

Our context has changed dramatically, and this has created a different change imperative today than there was even a year ago. Now there is much more appetite for disruption because of how we both individually and collectively adapted to the rapid changes we faced during the pandemic.

There is much more openness to change now than there has been in the past. The world of work is ever changing, but the changes have been dramatic and more rapid since the pandemic. At the same time, never before have agility and flexibility been so critical for workers trying to survive—and even grow—in their careers. There is a clear need for people to learn and reskill to keep up with the growing demands of this new world of work.

It is essential that workers today are mindful of their skill set. They must constantly learn, relearn, and adjust to the changes going on around them. In fact, the ability to be flexible and agile, while also continually learning and reskilling, is critical to ongoing success—both for employees and for the organizations they work for.

This is what the future of work is all about.

We have entered a new talent economy. We had been predicting it for the last five years, but the rapidly converging forces of the pandemic and the rolling waves of activism as a result of the #MeToo and Black Lives Matter movements have accelerated the need for change. There is unprecedented urgency to rethink our talent dynamics and the way we engage with our talent supply today.

I believe we have a collective social imperative right now to do better for our employees, to make more fair and inclusive people-resourcing decisions. There is a burning need to ensure

People practices, business practices, and strategic HR priorities must be better than those of the last decade.

we have reskilling for all people. I care deeply about everyone having a future and an opportunity to contribute their skills and talents to the workforce and economy. The risks of a disenfranchised generation or millions of people out of work are too great.

People practices, business practices, and strategic HR priorities must be better than those of the last decade. They must be more human centric, intelligent, more robust in their skills and capability matching, more learning- and growth-oriented, more enabling, more rigorous in their transparency and inclusivity, and better able to deliver the talent optimization that organizations will need in the coming decade.

In this book, we'll look closely at the current state of talent and HR practices to understand just why this change is so desperately and urgently needed. We'll listen to the voice of the people, seeing what employees are saying they want. We'll delve into the research Fuel50 and others have conducted to understand what the future of work must look like. We'll see what business thought leaders and experts are saying about what we need for a talent revolution. We'll look to the great change agents and revolutionary leaders of both history and the present day to learn what it takes to lead a successful revolution and create real change. And we'll explore what a blueprint for change can look like.

Along the way, you'll find case studies that share the real change missions of real companies who are clients of Fuel50, illustrating the objectives and strategies companies are articulating on their journeys through change.

And we'll be accompanied on our revolutionary journey by a very special young woman named Liberty, who will show us how true revolutionary change is born.

While we go on this journey, I have a task for you. Don't worry, it's a simple one—though not necessarily easy!

To effectively create change, you must know what you believe in. So as you read, I want you to consider these questions:

When you consider creating change in your organization,

- What is the experience you want to create within your organization?

- What difference do you want to make?

- What mark or impact do you want to leave on your organization?

- What are you willing to fight for?

- What are you willing to champion?

- What are your core beliefs?

- What are your nonnegotiables?

- What do you want to be remembered for within your organization?

- What do you want your legacy to be?

Keep these in your mind; we'll come back to them at the end of this book.

The time for the talent revolution is upon us. Let's begin our journey!

CHAPTER 1

Why We Need a Revolution

Liberty was a natural-born freedom fighter. She had grown up in a small village in a remote part of the highlands of a small Latin American country. She grew up living on the land and loved nothing more than a few days' hunting, hiking, and fishing with her five brothers. As the youngest of six siblings, she was used to working twice as hard to keep up with her brothers and to have her voice heard.

By the time she reached 18 years old, Liberty had begun to see clearly the inequities that surrounded her in her village. She saw the women who walked four miles every day to and from the closest stream to wash their families' clothes and collect water for the village. She heard them talk about struggling to feed their families. She heard their pain and concern about the diminished schooling for their children, as schools were closed for extended periods of time by the country's increasingly dictatorial government, which was putting more and more strict control measures into place. Meanwhile, the menfolk of the village sat around having council meetings and enjoying their chewing tobacco, addressing none of these issues.

Liberty was tired of all the talk but no action from the men and of the constant stream of angst and anxiety from the women, who were too exhausted from taking care of their families to take much action themselves. And she decided she was going to do something about it.

We are in the era of the democratization of the workforce.

Here is what I mean by that: think about the taxi industry. For decades, it operated more or less the same way. There was a particular path to being a taxi driver and a particular system for calling or hailing and taking a taxi.

Then along came Uber—and soon after, Lyft—and the taxi industry was irrevocably disrupted. All of a sudden, the marketplace opened wide. Anyone with a license (and a background check) could become an Uber driver, and riders could call an Uber from anywhere to anywhere, right from the comfort of a smartphone app. Uber democratized the rideshare marketplace for both drivers and riders.

The time has come to do the same thing in talent systems. It's time to disrupt the talent practices that have been entrenched for decades. It's time to democratize the talent marketplace, creating more opportunity and giving employees more control and autonomy over their career paths and future opportunities.

Just as Uber enables riders to customize their travel, helping them get from exactly where they are to exactly where they want to go, we can create a talent marketplace that helps employees do the same thing. And as Airbnb and Tripadvisor connect you to places you want to go, a talent marketplace connects people to a future.

And just as Uber and Lyft changed the power dynamic within the taxi industry, for better or worse, a talent marketplace will change the power dynamic for employees and the organizations they work for. It will be an adjustment as employees have more power to make their own choices, as they become more connected to all the opportunities before them. But this shift will ultimately benefit not just the employees but the organization, because it taps into an overlooked and underused source of talent: the employees already within an organization.

The Untapped Source of Talent

It's a question that organizations everywhere should be asking in today's chaotic business environment: *Why do so many organizations overlook their greatest source of talent—their own people?*

Deloitte first asked it well before the global pandemic and lockdown upended everyone's world,[1] and the question has only become more urgent as COVID-driven events have unfolded. But even before the 2020 lockdown, there was a growing disruption in jobs and necessary job skills that was being driven by changing technologies and new ways of working.

---

1   Robin Erickson, Denise Moulton, and Bill Cleary, "Are You Overlooking Your Greatest Source of Talent?" Deloitte Insights, July 30, 2018, https://www2.deloitte.com/us/en/insights/deloitte-review/issue-23/unlocking-hidden-talent-internal-mobility.html.

Numerous surveys tried to quantify the growing problem. McKinsey estimated that 14% of the global workforce, or as many as 375 million workers, would have to change jobs and/or acquire new skills in the next decade because of automation and artificial intelligence.[2] And yet, until now, most organizations have failed to react to this challenge, either because they lacked a sense of urgency or because they didn't have a plan for how to address the problem.

The global pandemic changed all of that—in a big way.

Suddenly organizations everywhere had to quickly adjust to rapid changes that were impacting and disrupting the global economy. A whole new set of business concepts that had been simmering on the back burner for many companies—things like flexibility, agility, mobility, and resilience—were now important elements that organizations everywhere were challenged to embrace if they wanted to grow and survive.

In a conversation I had with Brigin Walsh, strategic people change leader at Allied Irish Bank, she described it eloquently: "We no longer have the luxury of succession planning for the elite talent. We now need to face every day with a crisis response contingency plan for every single person on our team. We need to ensure our business stays open and our people remain healthy and safe during this crisis period we are facing."

The business publication *Forbes* succinctly described what needed to be done: "To succeed … organizations require a workforce that's agile and flexible. It's not enough to hire the best: to succeed organizations must also leverage and mobilize existing talent into new

---

2   Sapana Agrawal, Aaron De Smet, Sébastien Lacroix, and Angelika Reich, "COVID-19 and Reskilling the Workforce | McKinsey," McKinsey & Company, May 7, 2020, https://www.mckinsey.com/business-functions/organization/our-insights/to-emerge-stronger-from-the-covid-19-crisis-companies-should-start-reskilling-their-workforces-now.

roles, departments or offices. This mobility enables organizations to quickly meet changing business and market needs, increase efficiencies, unlock talent potential and future-proof their workforce."[3]

So how do you do that? How do you build a workforce that is both agile and flexible and that you can leverage into new roles and situations?

This dynamic remains even more critical as we enter an era of economic correction, with what is being dubbed full-employment recession, where we continue to face a talent shortage and low unemployment rates despite an economic correction. As Josh Bersin articulated it, "It doesn't look like a recession to me." Now we need to ensure, more than ever, that we have the best people in the right jobs, fully enabled to reskill for an unknown future, with accurate talent intelligence about the skills, talents, and capabilities of our people to ensure our organizations remain agile, resilient, and sustainable. A self-learning organization with agility at its core is as important in this era as it has ever been.[4]

Here's the answer: it's all about internal talent mobility, better leveraging your workforce, and making sure you have the right people, with the right skills, in the right place, at the right time.

WHAT IS INTERNAL TALENT MOBILITY?

Simply put, internal talent mobility is the process of moving people within your workforce to fill open opportunities. This can include

---

3   Rebecca Skilbeck, "Talent Mobility: The Key to Unlocking Your Organization's Potential," *Forbes*, May 30, 2019, https://www.forbes.com/sites/rebeccaskilbeck/2019/05/30/talent-mobility-the-key-to-unlocking-your-organizations-potential/.

4   Josh Bersin, "It Doesn't Look Like a Recession to Me," Josh Bersin, July 15, 2022, https://joshbersin.com/2022/07/it-doesnt-look-like-a-recession-to-me.

promotions to new roles, short-term redeployment, gig opportunities, or having people move to different departments.

But that's a very basic definition that probably doesn't do it justice.

What talent mobility really does is allow organizations to "dynamically develop and align their workforce to strategic business needs," as *Forbes* put it. "Moving beyond traditional succession planning, [talent] mobility allows HR professionals to proactively and strategically move people from role to role at any level of the business to meet organizational goals."[5] In other words, internal talent mobility is an essential part of every organization's talent development.

There are two important reasons why internal talent mobility makes sense in today's rapidly changing business environment. First, leveraging your existing talent can be a great way to build organizational and personal resilience while maintaining productivity and saving money, time, and resources. And second, promoting internal talent mobility encourages cross-team talent sharing and cultivates a culture of learning and development. People who have a growth mindset—a passion for continuous learning and an expanding skill set—are better able to embrace change with greater confidence.

Talent mobility also enables organizations to rapidly adapt to changing environments, with the ability to deploy and move key skills across projects, across the business, and across borders when needed. Mobility provides avenues for staff to progress and evolve within an organization and can lead to 30% better processes and 23% more productivity overall.[6] Plus, it encourages employees to stay with the

---

5   Ibid.

6   *2015 Executive Enterprise Mobility Report,* CITO Research, 2015, https://techorchard. com/wp-content/uploads/2015/02/2015_Executive_EnterpriseMobility_Survey.pdf.

company and grow their career within their current organization, and that is a win-win proposition for everyone.

AND YET ...

Despite all of these benefits, although internal talent mobility is being embraced by more organizations in 2021, the numbers show that many still have not embraced it completely. For example, a recent Human Capital Institute (HCI) pulse survey found that only "61% of respondents' organizations have a policy to first search internally to fill an open position before posting the job externally." As promising as that sounds, HCI still found that nearly 4 out of 10 organizations (39%) *don't* require that hiring managers search for internal job candidates first before looking at outside applicants.[7]

For the last decade or more, recruiting new talent from outside the organization was the default position for a great many companies whenever there was an internal opening. Although recruiting outside talent is an essential part of improving any business, many companies seemed to overlook or ignore promising talent already in their employ, operating right under their nose.

Equally problematic was an overemphasis on recruiting new employees, which frequently frustrated current employees

There's more going on behind the scenes than what you may see—and it starts with the entrenched systemic traditions that have long been the bedrock of how HR operates.

---

7   Human Capital Institute, "Optimize Internal Talent Mobility Strategies in 2021," January 27, 2021, https://www.hci.org/webcast/optimize-internal-talent-mobility-strategies-2021.

when they saw new people get hired for positions in their own organization they never knew were available. The common lament heard in the HR world is that it's easier to find a job on LinkedIn than it is within your own organization. Company culture and employee engagement suffered as a result, and the failure to optimize the potential of current employees was not only discouraging but often pushed a great many workers to seek employment elsewhere.

So, if internal talent mobility is so great, why is it not the norm? Because there's more going on behind the scenes than what you may see—and it starts with the entrenched systemic traditions that have long been the bedrock of how HR operates.

The Hierarchical Career Model

About two years ago, I met with a big company in New York. We were talking about their talent strategies and how they support their employees' careers within the organization. The HR person sat down and told me, "Here, an employee does not own their career. Here, your manager owns your career. The way we do career management is that nothing will happen unless your manager advocates for you." Very intentionally and clearly, they said that employees do not have any opportunities unless their manager puts them forward. The manager controls their career experience. Without manager advocacy, nothing will happen to your career or your future within that organization.

I've never in my life walked out of a meeting with anyone thinking, "I don't think I want to work with this organization unless there is a radical change in their mindset." But let me tell you, this shaped my resolve to create an even better career experience for employees around the globe, where employees could own their future and control their destiny and take ownership for their own careers.

Now, this incident is an outlier. We don't often hear companies articulate this kind of mindset. Most organizations do put at least some thought into how to create career mobility and career growth for their people. But as the numbers we cited show, many organizations are still entrenched in the old ways. Even if it's not explicit, the way it was at that New York organization, it is hard to excise the systemic patterns that have been entrenched in organizations for decades.

In our recent report on driving employee engagement through career development, Fuel50 found that "50% of HR Leaders said their per employee career development spend was below USD $1K (or between 0 and 3% of salary). Notably, only a third of respondents believe their organization invests adequately in employee development, with 35% stating that their organization should be investing more."[8]

Even among organizations that offer employee training, the focus is generally only on high-intensity training for a few elite employees. The standard model is to look after your so-called critical talent rather than offer growth and training to every employee.

This approach is based in the traditional model of succession planning. The word *succession* immediately conjures images of hierarchy, from the monarchs of history who placed so much stake in what heir would inherit the throne to countless tales of battles for the seat of power. It's a tale as old as time that is still relevant today, one we see recreated everywhere from HBO's current hit *Succession*, which follows a family media empire and the battle over who will take over the company, back to Shakespeare's *King Lear*, on which it is based, all the way back to the earliest plays of the Greeks. There's a

---

8   *Global Talent Mobility Research Reports—Part 6: Current Talent Mobility Practices, Imperatives and Best Practices*, Fuel50, February 2022, https://fuel50.com/research/global-talent-mobility/.

reason why contemporary productions of Shakespeare's plays about kings and succession are so often set in corporations: the hierarchical succession planning in companies is a direct descendant of the succession planning of monarchs through the ages.

That same monarchical structure creates a culture whereby the "elite" get opportunities other employees don't. Just as the kings of old had their lords and knights, their elite talent, leadership in organizations tend to have their favorites. While job vacancies are starting to become more open and transparent, there is still a real lack of transparency around stretch assignments and projects. Often employees are left saying, "How did that person get on that project? I would have loved to contribute to that. How do I get considered for projects like that?" All too often, leadership and management play favorites, tapping certain people for those projects or positions without ever opening up the opportunity to the wider organization.

People come into the workplace with inherent privilege or lack of privilege. This can become a self-perpetuating cycle, with the privileged rising and rising while the less privileged never have the same opportunities. Someone who went to the same private alma mater as the CEO may get tapped for more opportunities because of that connection, while someone who is equally talented and maybe even more interested in those opportunities is overlooked because they went to a public university. If an employee has a family connection to someone in leadership or management, they may be given preferential treatment and more opportunities to advance their career.

This elitism has historically also existed in talent-cultivation strategies where only elite talent received training and development investment as part of "high-potential" or acceleration programs. This elitist thinking is outdated today. If you want business outcomes like better engagement, retention, and even productivity per employee, organizations need to develop a democratic talent strategy where all employees are invested. This is the only way to future-proof the skills of the workforce to be more competitive in the future.

Even beyond lack of equal opportunity for all, the traditional model of succession planning is inherently flawed, because it never really considers what the employee wants. There isn't much real conversation about what the employee considers to be the best move for their career, for their aspirations, desires, talents, growth goals. There's no alignment. The model is one sided and top down.

As Josh Bersin writes, "If you were a scientist or engineer (like me), and you never wanted to move into management, you pretty much had to deal with it. Maybe your company had a good technical career track, but maybe it didn't."[9]

If you are focused on your hierarchy, on your succession planning, you end up squeezing people into boxes regardless of what they want. HR makes the decision behind closed doors rather than in communication with the employee involved. The conversation tends to be, "Hey, you're getting promoted into this position! Congratulations!" with no discussion of what the employee considers to be the best move for themself.

While some companies in the past few decades started to pay more attention to what their employees actually want in their careers, as Bersin writes, "they baked the 'career development' process into performance management. Your managers, the sacrosanct owner of your life at work, was supposed to help you manage your career. This concept became very embedded in companies, so much so that many of the companies I see tell me 'we don't encourage people to shop for

---

9   Josh Bersin, "Career Management Goes Mission Critical: And It's All about to Change," Josh Bersin, June 18, 2019, https://joshbersin.com/2019/06/career-management-goes-mission-critical-and-its-all-about-to-change/.

new jobs unless their manager approves.'" This system, Bersin writes, "holds everyone back. Not only are managers often unaware of other opportunities in a company, but most of them aren't that good at coaching people in the first place. (Being a career coach is quite a sophisticated role.)"[10]

Even if it isn't blatantly stated, as it was in that organization in New York, in the old hierarchical model, somebody makes a decision on your behalf. Your career trajectory within an organization is very controlled. The traditional hierarchical system is very linear and very structured. There is one path for you, whether you want it or not. It is a very top-down approach, and the decisions tend to be made behind closed doors.

This linear, structured system is a remnant of the structured, controlled assembly lines of the Henry Ford industrialized era. This was a system of production in which every employee had a tightly defined unit of work to do. While literal assembly lines were a staple of manual factory labor, this same ethos bled into the general workplace: every employee had a strictly delineated job and was expected to stay in their spot and do that job as instructed by management.

In the past, it might have been acceptable to have the managers and the top echelons of the company control everyone's careers and orchestrate career paths. In the past, it might have been acceptable for leadership to tap their favorites, their "elite" talent, for training and opportunities. But those days are over. The days of having an elite talent structure are coming to an end. The old model of succession planning is coming to an end. Those old models are ripe for disruption. We are entering the age of the free market—something very different from what Henry Ford conceptualized.

---

10   Ibid.

Just as the American revolutionaries overthrew the British monarchical forces in favor of a democratic system, the time has come to overturn the hierarchical talent structure of old in favor of a free, open, and democratic talent marketplace.

The Marketplace

Going forward, talent mobility needs to be enabled by a marketplace. We are in an era of shifting from manager-led growth to marketplace-led growth. We've seen these marketplace solutions in other areas, with platforms like eBay, which connects people to things they want to buy; LinkedIn and Facebook, which connect people to people; and Uber, Tripadvisor, and Airbnb, which connect people to places they want to go. A talent marketplace connects people to opportunities within their business. The goal of an internal talent marketplace program is to create a free labor market within the organization in which everybody has the opportunity to participate, as opposed to the traditional hierarchical structures in which everyone has their set place and trajectory.

Of course, this revolution, like all revolutions, is not without its challenges. Some of these challenges are because of additional ingrained practices, like talent hoarding—another dirty HR secret nobody likes to talk about.

TALENT HOARDING

Talent hoarding is the antithesis of talent mobility. A talent hoarder is someone who holds people in place longer than they should, risking stagnation, plateauing, and boredom through lack of growth and opportunity. Some leaders and managers just want to hold on to their talent. They've got somebody who is up to speed, who knows what they're doing, who is valuable to their department. And the head of that department doesn't want to share that resource with any other part of the business.

The reason for this goes back to the managerial workplace structure. "Managers are held accountable for business results," Josh Bersin explains. "If your best person leaves your group to go elsewhere in the company, it may make your job harder—so if the reward system is not designed to facilitate such mobility, you as a manager are going to hold them back."[11]

If you keep someone on your team, not letting them grow and advance in their career, you can pretend it's not going to happen, but eventually that person is going to get frustrated. They're going to look elsewhere to grow their skills and move forward. And most likely, they're going to look outside of your organization.

The opposite of a talent hoarder is a talent agent. If you become a great talent nurturer, a great talent coach, you're going to attract more talent. If other people see the employees working for you getting all these opportunities, you will become a talent agent—giving employees the agency to grow the careers they want. You'll be the kind of leader people want to work for.

If you can grow, foster, and share talent, you have a much greater chance of retaining that talent within the company. If people see growth within your team, they're going to want to work with you. If they see the people in your team growing and developing and getting opportunities, they will want to be part of that team. And if the company's reputation develops as a place with great talent development and talent growth, you are going to attract more people. Your talent pipeline will grow and self-perpetuate.

---

11   Ibid.

THE FLATLINE CAREER

Another challenge is the newly flattened structure many organizations have created. The old structural model resembled a staircase. As an employee, every few years you had an opportunity to move up a step. You could move your way up an organization and receive lots of training and education along the way that prepared you for future steps.

Today, many organizations have a flattened structure. Many companies have taken out layers of management, so there is not vertical trajectory. There are no opportunities for promotion. As such, organizations struggle with how to enable employees to grow and advance in their careers.

This means careers are characterized by a flatline, a plateau that lasts for a significant period of time. And when there is a vertical, it's often massive. Today's early career experience is characterized by a longer period at the front line, more time at the coalface, nose to the grindstone, less promotion, fewer vertical rises, and less opportunity to grow your skills through those advances that once existed. You haven't had those interstitial steps along the way that provided the learning and experience to prepare you for that vertical promotion. Without that preparation, those sudden, steep verticals can lead to career derailment.

Companies need to ask, How do you keep people engaged and growing through those periods? How do you restructure your organization so people can deliver work and complete projects and grow as they complete those projects? How do you shift your organization in terms of the way work is delivered and enabled?

During those longer runs, organizations need to give employees a sense of momentum, providing opportunities for growth and learning, offering stretch assignments and experiences and projects that build skills, creating a sense of career growth during those flat stretches. This creates a more engaged internal society. A key focus during these longer runs should be on skill development, so that during this plateau period employees can still achieve career momentum and acceleration in preparation for the future. In the old world, job titles were the dominant career currency. Skills and expertise are the career currency of the future—and this currency can be increased even while an employee is in the same job for a longer period of time.

WHOSE RESPONSIBILITY?

There's also the challenge of ownership. If one end of the spectrum is complete managerial/leadership control of an employee's career, on the other end of the spectrum are the organizations that say, "Yes, our employees own their own careers"—and then provide literally zero support for mobility and growth within the company. This is the cop-out end of the spectrum: companies saying, "Your career is your responsibility; it has nothing to do with us. It's all up to you. We're taking no part in it."

Again, this is the extreme end of the spectrum. But all too often, organizations simply give lip service to the idea of employees owning their careers without offering any support. After all, it's so much easier to say, "It's your career. It's your responsibility. You go and find a course at a university somewhere to learn new skills." This is not done with malicious intent. Companies simply don't know what to do or how to do it. It feels too hard. But if you want employees to own their careers, the organization must enable those employees to grow and advance, giving them opportunities to develop their careers within the organization.

So who should take ownership of and responsibility for talent cultivation and development? Too often, it's like a game of hot potato.

"It's management's problem. No, it's leadership's problem. No, it's the employees' problem." Nobody wants to take responsibility.

The truth is, it must be a three-way partnership between the organization, the leadership, and the employee—a shared responsibility between all of the parties.

THE DECONSTRUCTION CHALLENGE

And finally, of course, it can feel difficult—even impossible—for organizations to unbundle and deconstruct what they've built, to dismantle the traditional talent system, especially if it's been in place for decades. It feels like pushing a boulder up a hill. In the realm of HR, change is incredibly slow. It can be a long, challenging process for leaders to get on board and to grant a budget for anything discretionary. Historically, remodeling the architecture of a company is time consuming and cumbersome. It could be a three-to-five-year project, and it could cost millions.

But today, we have a powerful force on our side: artificial intelligence. Today, we have the opportunity to use AI to create agile architectures that morph as your organization is radically changed day to day—as we've seen happening during the pandemic, supporting workforce agility.

AI can help address many of the biggest hurdles that stand in the way of internal mobility success. When asked, *"What is the top internal mobility challenge at your organization?"* HCI's survey listed the top four "extreme barriers" that more than one in five respondents said were holding back internal mobility in their organizations:

- Lack of a database of searchable, comprehensive talent profiles (26% of respondents agreed),

- Lack of a strategic workforce plan for identifying critical roles and skill gaps (26%),

- Lack of effective technology to manage the process (23%), and

- Managers not developing their team members/giving them feedback (22%).[12]

All of these challenges we've discussed may seem daunting, but there is a powerful tool that can help this revolution take hold: the talent marketplace platform. A talent marketplace platform creates a free and open marketplace that helps address all of these challenges.

A Revolutionary Dream

Fuel50 was born out of a revolutionary dream to create such a platform, which could transform legacy talent systems into democratic talent marketplaces where employees and organizations are connected in a fair, equitable manner supporting the concept of equal talent citizenship—a marketplace approach that creates an opportunity to exchange talent and skills for reward, remuneration, and opportunity.

My personal fascination with career matching started when I was 14, when I took a short paper-and-pencil career test and it told me I should either be a vocational guidance counselor or a funeral director. Those were my number one and two career options, according to the test: funeral director or vocational guidance counselor!

"Okay," I thought, "where is the commonality between these two careers? And how the heck did the test match my skills and talents to these seemingly random occupations?"

---

12   Human Capital Institute.

That fascination never stopped. I started my university studies with a dream of creating a better career test than the one I took at 14. I studied psychology because I saw it as the field that would best help me achieve that dream.

After university, my first step in following this dream was a job as a career guidance counselor. I really enjoyed the position, but I became increasingly frustrated with the methodologies and tools people were using in that field. Three degrees later, I was trained in holistic nondirectional counseling, which meant we took into consideration all aspects of a person when considering their career choices, not just their education or training. People would come to us and say, "Can you help me make a better career decision?" and the process could be quite intimate; we really wanted to get to know who people were at their deepest level.

I believe people need data and information to make great decisions. But the career tests available back then were pretty weak and not as useful as a test could be. In fact, by the time I was working, testing had gone completely out of favor. And yet career testing still fascinated me, even though it was quite unfashionable. I still had my dream of creating a better career test that could help people understand where they could best use their talents. So after my stint as a career guidance counselor, I did a further degree in psychology, completed my master's, and became a registered organizational psychologist.

The next 15 to 20 years of my career were spent building predictive psychometric tests that matched people to jobs, primarily in a business I started called Talent Technologies. By the early 2000s, in my spare time I had built a career-matching experience that we called the Online Career Centre, which took a holistic approach developed for our coaching business called Career Analysts. It wasn't just matching skills and talents to jobs; it also looked at your values, your interests, your experiences. It was whole-person matching.

The Talent Technologies business of psychometric prediction was doing extremely well. We had become New Zealand's number one psychometric assessment provider. The science was fundamentally the same; it was still matching talent to jobs. But the tests became so powerful that you could take 1,000 people and run them to see if they matched a particular job, and 997 would have an X next to their name, with only three bearing a check mark. That's how good the science became. You could pick 3 future performers out of 1,000 based on this data.

The science was incredible—and in demand too. But it still wasn't fulfilling my mission, my dream. In fact, I was becoming more and more frustrated and disillusioned. "This is not my purpose in life," I thought. "I didn't study and work for 28 years so that I could play God with people's lives by putting exes or check marks next to their names." I hated it. I knew we could do better.

That point became a personal pivot moment to focus on the career-matching business, and I invited one of my colleagues, Jo Mills, to become the cofounder of Fuel50, which was by then taking our career-matching technology to global businesses like Citigroup and Westpac. We knew we weren't finished with our mission. We knew we could do more with career matching, allowing people to use their talent and potential, empowering individuals to see what their opportunities are, what the best fit is—not just from the organization's perspective but from their perspective as an individual.

I'd spent 20 years of my career creating tests that were from the perspective of the employer. Now we wanted to create a career-matching experience that was from the perspective of the *employee*. Our mission was to create a test that served the individual, not just the organization.

We realized we could take the same powerful science and reapply it for a better purpose—and that's how Fuel50 was born. We took the science used in the psychometric tests and reverse engineered it—something that had never been done before. Rather than putting the power into the hands of the organization, it puts the power into the hands of the employee, to see where their talents and skills fit best, where they could take their careers, and their best fit opportunities, and to build a road map to their future.

A New Model

Our dream, our mission, has always been to help people make great decisions about their career and their future. Now we have the incredible technological advances to be able to do that. The Fuel50 platform creates a free and open marketplace that allows people to personalize their career, plan for the future, connect with mentors, find projects, build skills, and see what opportunities are available across the organization.

Our model is about creating opportunities for everyone to find, develop, and play to their best talents. We want to create a more democratic experience where everyone is contributing equally and where everyone has the opportunity to contribute to the talent economy. We want a free and equal labor market within organizations.

Our dream, our mission, has always been to help people make great decisions about their career and their future. And to enable them to make their future a reality.

My dream, with my cofounder, Jo Mills, and our team of over 100 Fuellies, is for Fuel50 to enable and empower individuals to find the best fit opportunity for them, their talent, their passion, and their aspirations. It asks, What is your best fit across this organization? Where do you want to be, and how can you get there? If you can find out where your talent best fits, you'll be more valuable and productive and, most importantly, happier and have more opportunity to contribute your skills and talents in a passion-aligned way.

Fuel50 comes from the philosophical lens that you can do anything—and it tells you how you can make it happen. It doesn't sugarcoat the fact that it may take a lot of work to get where you want to go. But it gives you actionable steps to get there.

Say you dream of becoming the CEO. Fuel50 will never say, "No, that's impossible." What it will say is, "You have a current CEO-score match of 15%. Here are the skills you need to build in order to become a closer match for the CEO position. Here are the 10 steps you need to take to get you closer to that dream. You need to take this course on business acumen, this course on marketing strategy, this course on reading a profit and loss. Here are some stretch assignments and projects to grow those skills. Here is a mentor in your organization who is three steps ahead of you, who can help coach you on your way." And it will list what you need to do to progress on that path toward CEO—or whatever other role appeals to you.

Fuel50 can also help you see whether the position you *think* you want is actually what you want. I used to think I would make a great chief people officer (CPO). I put that into Fuel50's system, and it only gave me a 60% match score. I was surprised—but then I looked at my skill gaps. The gaps were in areas like risk and compliance and employee contracts. "Oh yeah," I said. "I'm not really interested in those areas. So CPO actually is probably not the best fit for me." The system gave me the information to make the decision of whether to pursue that position—and if so, what steps I needed to take—or whether I should actually pursue a different trajectory.

I put what I was interested in doing into the Fuel50 marketplace, and the matches it gave me were positions involving change and transformation or organizational strategy—a much better fit for me. That is a journey I would potentially take.

The purpose of Fuel50 is to be empowering, to never say no, but to also give a reality check in terms of what you need to do to make your dream come true by creating a fair, democratic, inclusive marketplace for your skills and talents.

Freedom, Equality, Democracy

With a free and open talent marketplace within an organization, opportunities are transparent and available to everyone. If the organization offers the same support to everyone, talent will grow and the organization will benefit. Fuel50's AI makes this possible. It makes growth and training scalable across the entire organization, allowing you to enable each and every employee to participate rather than focus only on high-intensity training for a few elite employees.

A free talent marketplace democratizes the hierarchical system. The people who are traditionally at the "bottom" of the hierarchy—the employees—are given power over their careers, and the people "above" them in the hierarchy—managers and leaders—support them. It's a shift to a more equal partnership model.

And in our experience, it's what people at every level of the organization want. Leaders want to be able to see what reskilling is available to their people. They want the ability to connect people to those reskilling opportunities, projects, stretch assignments, and coaching or mentors. Managers want to be able to get coaching tips to their people. They want to be able to say, "Here are three things you could be doing right now to get where you want to go." Employees want to have ownership of their careers—and they want the tools to be able to own and grow their future.

In an open talent market, every employee is a free agent. Everyone can come and go and market their skills. This creates freedom for everyone: for employees in having ownership over their careers, and in giving employees ownership, it creates freedom for managers and leaders, who are now not solely responsible for their employees' career advancement.

A democratized talent economy enables more people to be at their best, to develop the skills the organization needs. A free and open talent marketplace says, "We are all citizens in the economy of the organization." And it creates an equitable society where everybody gets to pursue their career aspirations.

There's risk associated with not improving your talent experience within your organization. If you don't create a growth culture, you risk not being able to achieve your innovation or competitive goals. You want your people hungry, engaged, motivated, excited, energized about the future. In the old hierarchical structure, the only form of motivation was, "Climb the ladder! Get a promotion!" which could lead to a position someone may not be interested in or passionate about. It's far more motivating to know that you're working toward something you love, something you're really excited and passionate about, something you truly want to do.

It's Time for the Talent Revolution

Deloitte cut to the heart of the issue when they wrote the following:

The business opportunity is clear-cut. First, you can avoid replacement and recruitment costs incurred when people leave. But even greater is the opportunity to reshape your employment brand and workplace culture. Many of today's youngest workers are eager to build their careers rapidly and want to work for organizations that challenge them and promote them quickly.

Internal mobility—how that happens—is not just a way to retain talent. It also helps to create a powerful magnet for people outside your organization who seek professional growth. The result? The talent market can see your organization as one that champions ambition and performance in everything it does. Think about what kind of talent you'll attract and keep—whether inside or outside your organization.[13]

And it was the late, great Walt Disney who observed that, "Times and conditions change so rapidly that we must keep our aim constantly focused on the future." He was right, of course, because expending meaningful effort and energy creating experiences and expectations for talent that encourage growth, learning, engagement, and communication demonstrates to employees that you're committed to investing in their future with you. As a result, time to hire and costs decrease, while employee engagement and retention will increase.

A company is nothing without its employees, without its people—and the voice of the people is something that can no longer be ignored.

---

13   Robin Erickson, Denise Moulton, and Bill Cleary, "Are You Overlooking Your Greatest Source of Talent?" Deloitte Insights, July 30, 2018, https://www2.deloitte.com/us/en/insights/deloitte-review/issue-23/unlocking-hidden-talent-internal-mobility.html.

CUSTOMER JOURNEYS THROUGH CHANGE

Case Study A

> **Organization: A multinational British company that is one of the world's largest suppliers of enterprise resource planning customers. It has 6.1 million customers worldwide and offices in 24 countries and employs more than 12,000 employees around the world.**

We currently see capability gaps in managing, measuring, and supporting internal mobility, identifying and supporting required skills and capabilities across regions/functions, enabling career pathing and planning, and succession planning.

We want to adhere to our values of transparency and doing the right thing.

We expect the opportunity marketplace (OMP) to be a game changer for colleagues across the business, empowering them to understand the skills they possess today, the skills required to move forward in the existing role or future roles, while supporting them to access appropriate learning, coaching, and project opportunities to realize these ambitions.

We also want to allow HR and leaders across the business to have visibility across the in-house talent pool, to see talent shortages before they impact the business, and to see and proactively manage high-performing colleagues, talent pools, skill aging, competitor advantage, and successors.

We currently do not have a consistent approach to capability/skill identification, taxonomy, or management. There is limited formal succession planning in place below the senior leadership teams. Job description governance has to date not been a high priority.

The integration with our current HR ecosystem should be designed with a core aim of providing an efficient candidate and colleague experience; engaging and nurturing talent; supporting the acquisition and development of skills/capability; and the wider ecosystem of data, analytics, and systems.

KEY DELIVERABLES FOR THE OMP INCLUDE

- Increasing the ability to proactively provision talent, skills, and capability;

- Reducing "reactivity" to providing staffing and coverage for key areas of the business;

- Reducing the need for contract and contingent workers;

- Giving employees visibility of future career opportunities, development opportunities, and stable employment to persuade them to stay in the face of external opportunities;

- Executing on HR's top priority for 2021–22: right people, right place, and enabling critical skills and competency development (and skills versatility) through experiential learning; and

- Saving future recruiting time and costs and increasing speed to productivity for new team members or those in a new role.

CHAPTER 2

The Voice of the People: Understanding What Your People Want

"Never underestimate the power of listening to people."

Liberty was going to take matters into her own hands. But she knew she needed to learn more about the problems her village was having and how they should be addressed. In order to learn this, she needed to talk to the people around her. So she created a listening plan to learn from all the different sectors of her community, segmenting the voices of the people around her so she could understand what there was to learn and what could be done from all the different perspectives in her community.

She spoke to women who kept the village fed and running like clockwork. She spoke to the elders who created the rules. She spoke to the young adults and even to the children. She even decided to include those outside the village who passed through from time to time—travelers, traders, even aid and missionary workers—to understand their perspective on what was happening around her.

She learned that each segment of her community had a different perspective, a nuanced outlook on the situation they were facing, a personalized view and story of what they were collectively experiencing: food shortages, outdated leadership, a culture of fear of the outside world.

The employee voice has never been stronger than it is today. Organizations have no choice now but to be above reproach in the way they are treating their people. How do we anticipate these events will impact the world of work?

We have seen the pendulum swing dramatically from a world where employers had the balance of power to a power dynamic that favors employees.

We have seen the pendulum swing dramatically from a world where employers had the balance of power to a power dynamic that favors employees. As organizations delayered and restructured in the last two decades, in the new decade we are actually experiencing a global talent shortage. The catch cry now is all about employee retention, employee voice, and the need to create great employee experiences that will retain talent. The 2020s is the era of the Great Resignation, and our 2021 Talent Mobility Research is showing that up to 50% of employees are actively looking for another role.

In the last five years, we have seen a massive shift in talent supply-demand economics, where employee voice and sentiment are of vital importance. This has radically accelerated since the pandemic. The talent shortage means that organizations now need to rapidly reskill their workforce. Just about every tech company is trying to build an operating model or a framework to make its products future-ready. The goal today is to make sure that our clients can utilize their technology solutions to help them tackle both the problems of today *and* the problems of tomorrow. We are finding accelerated demand right now for an agile workforce and for a talent marketplace solution that supports workforce agility, reskilling, and the delivery of an inclusive career experience for all employees that is based on principles of fairness and transparency.

The fact is, when this support is not offered by the organizations, employees start taking matters into their own hands. This trend predates the pandemic: our 2015 Fuel50 Career Agility Research showed that 31% of employees want to accelerate or fast-track their careers, 35% want more work responsibilities and believe they can contribute more, and 75% would use their own time to further their career and take on additional learning that would benefit them at work.

Most employees today think they have more skills, talent, and potential than their employers are using. Fuel50's 2021 Talent Mobility data shows that employees are even more inclined to take matters into their own hands today, getting on with their own reskilling. Eighty percent of employees surveyed agreed that they took personal responsibility to seek out learning experiences and development opportunities for themselves rather than waiting for their organization to provide for them.

I take the initiative to seek out development opportunities and learning experiences myself

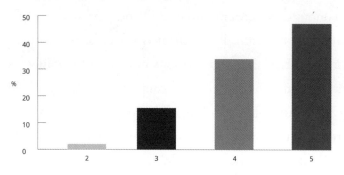

Source: Fuel50, Global Talent Mobility Best Practice Research

At the same time, only 21% of employees agreed that there was any compensation provided by their organization for acquiring and developing new skills.

I am compensated or rewarded for acquiring and developing new skills

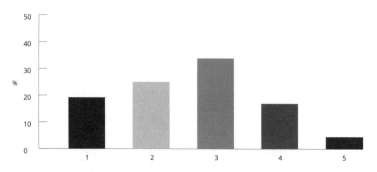

Source: Fuel50, Global Talent Mobility Best Practice Research

"There is no going back to the way talent looks at how they experience work," Larry McAlister, vice president of global talent at

NetApp, said in response to a question we asked about the future of work. "My vision is to enable through technology and leadership to have everyone feel they are doing their best work of their career at NetApp from their kitchen table. Closing the gap and understanding our employees' passions, skills, and career desires and then ensuring we are matching them to their next greatest opportunity. We need to be brave and take chances on growth and opportunity. We can't assume there is a perfect candidate in the external marketplace when we already have someone ready to make a career leap internally."

Fuel50's research findings on talent mobility are corroborated by other studies and surveys. A May 2021 article in the *Harvard Business Review* reported the findings of a study conducted by Citrix, which found that "82% of employees and 62% of HR directors believe that workers will need to reskill or upskill at least once a year to maintain a competitive advantage in a global job market." The majority of employees (73%) and HR directors (72%) believe that technology is key to breaking down hierarchies within organizations. The majority of employees (83%) and HR directors (67%) also believe that a flexible working future will enable unprecedented "career agility." In fact, 88% of employees say that when looking for new positions, they search for organizations that have the latest collaborative technology in place to enable agile learning. HR directors also consider this the most important factor in recruiting and retaining the best talent.[14]

The Impact of COVID

COVID-19 has starkly underlined the need for a talent revolution, as we saw the world of work entirely upended. In June of 2020, the

---

14   Tim Minahan, "What Your Future Employees Want Most," *Harvard Business Review*, May 31, 2021, https://hbr.org/2021/05/what-your-future-employees-want-most.

World Bank predicted that the global economy would shrink by 5.2% following the coronavirus pandemic and the shutdown measures to contain it. This would have a direct impact on investments, human capital development (loss of work/schooling), and fragmentation of global trade and supply linkages. According to the World Bank, "In 2021, the average incomes of people in the bottom 40 percent of the global income distribution are 6.7 percent lower than pre-pandemic projections, while those of people in the top 40 percent are down 2.8 percent."[15] We saw in real time that how successfully a business responds and devises strategies to minimize the impact of COVID-19 determines whether they will remain in business or have to close their doors for good, adding to the shrinking of the economy and the increase in unemployment and poverty. I certainly know that on the high street where I live, it seems every third business has shut its doors in the last two years.

We have all been impacted by the outbreak of COVID-19, which has, more than ever before, forced organizations to respond at pace, disregarding well-thought-out business strategies and implementing new directions overnight. This has sent ripples through operational, financial, and employer-employee relationships—and it has changed the employee experience forever. People's perspectives on what is important to them in their work has changed dramatically, with a new emphasis on flexibility and the importance of connection with others. And, more than ever, employees are demanding their voices be heard.

---

15   Carolina Sanchez-Paramo, Ruth Hill, Daniel Gerszon Mahler, Ambar Narayan, and Nishant Yonzan, "COVID-19 Leaves a Legacy of Rising Poverty and Widening Inequality," *World Bank Blogs* (blog), October 7, 2021, https://blogs.worldbank.org/developmenttalk/covid-19-leaves-legacy-rising-poverty-and-widening-inequality.

THE OVERNIGHT PIVOT TO REMOTE WORK

In March 2020, organizations were forced to transition to remote working practices virtually overnight. Teams, functions, service delivery models, and supply-chain logistics had to be transformed to ensure the organization could keep its doors open and delivering to customers. The Fuel50 June 2020 Capabilities Research paper showed that two of the top capabilities that trended during the pandemic were supply-chain resilience and strategic cost management.

We reached out to some of the companies we work with to ask for their views on the changing talent marketplace. Brigin Walsh, strategic people change leader at Allied Irish Bank (AIB), said future trends of work have accelerated by 10 years during the pandemic. "At AIB, we are not using the term 'remote' as we experience this new era," Walsh said. "We have to be careful that our people don't feel remote from the business, particularly in this era."

THE COLLECTIVE PEOPLE CHALLENGE

Collectively, HR and business leaders faced increased and unprecedented challenges because of operating in the pandemic era. As Marylene Delbourg-Delphis put it, chief people officers had the most important job in the business, even more important than that of many chief financial officers.[16]

The challenges included the following:

- **Remote working.** There has been a dramatic shift from employees working in the office to working remotely.

---

16 Jessica Miller-Merrell, "Driving Organizational Change: Rebuilding Trust and Culture." Workology, October 17, 2018, https://workology.com/ep-155-driving-organizational-change-rebuilding-trust-and-culture/.

- **Digital leadership.** Managers and leaders had to drive engagement, organizational culture, and connection to the overall business remotely.

- **Increased uncertainty.** There has been widespread uncertainty for organizations and the workforce financially, economically, and health-wise.

- **Reduced employee interaction and connection.** People have lost opportunities to interact in person with their leaders, business unit, fellow employees, and the larger organization.

Top Findings on the Impact of COVID

In 2021, the Fuel50 Global Talent Mobility Benchmarking Study asked HR leaders and employees from over 200 organizations across the globe a series of questions to explore the impact of the global pandemic on organizations and people practices. Three big findings on the impact of COVID on workforce and HR practices across the globe emerged from our research.

KEY FINDING 1: THE BIG FREEZE IS BEHIND US, AND WE NOW FACE "THE GREAT RESIGNATION"

When Fuel50 asked HR leaders how their organization responded initially to the pandemic, almost all said they reacted to COVID by instituting a recruitment freeze at some stage in 2020, and 40% of respondents said they stopped all recruitment activity in Q2 of 2020.

However, our findings show that the big freeze is behind us, as recruitment numbers now are predicted to be equal, if not higher, than before the pandemic. Sixty-three percent of respondents said they believe their recruitment numbers will show an increase over 2020 numbers. Our research found that despite the widespread recruitment freezes in 2020, there is now a returned business confidence demonstrated by the fact that the recruitment numbers have increased.

It is also worth noting that, according to *Forbes*, talent mobility programs have had a proven positive impact on employee retention, with a 60% reduction in attrition where a talent marketplace is used by employees,[17] as we predicted in our Career Engagement Benchmarking research conducted in 2015.[18]

Recruitment Activities

Q2 2020

40% of respondents said they stopped all recruitment activity in Q2 of 2020

Q2 2021

63% of respondents said they believe their recruitment numbers for 2020 will show an increase over 2020 numbers

Source: Fuel50, Global Talent Mobility Best Practice Research

---

17   Holly Corbett, "The Great Resignation: Why Employees Don't Want to Go Back to the Office," *Forbes*, July 28, 2021, https://www.forbes.com/sites/hollycorbett/2021/07/28/the-great-resignation-why-employees-dont-want-to-go-back-to-the-office/.

18   "Career Engagement Benchmarking," Fuel50, 2015, https://www.fuel50.com/resources/career-engagement-benchmarking/.

KEY FINDING 2: BOTH PRODUCTIVITY AND QUALITY TRENDED UP DURING THE PANDEMIC

Despite the pandemic and the challenges of remote working, 90% of HR respondents either saw productivity remain the same or increase, with nearly 40% seeing productivity gains. A quarter of respondents even said they saw an increase in the quality of work over the 2020–2021 period.

In line with our finding of increased productivity, a survey by Airtasker found that flexible workers on average work 1.4 more days every month than traditional office workers. That's 16.8 more days per year.[19]

But there are some common reasons why organizations generally have resisted moving to remote working, which an article published by *Forbes* cites. These include loss of organizational credibility from not having an office space for client meetings, reduced access to employees for urgent tasks and conversations, and reduced productivity from employees distracted by chores and children.[20]

---

19   "The Benefits of Working from Home," *Airtasker* (blog), March 31, 2020, https://www. airtasker.com/blog/the-benefits-of-working-from-home/.

20   Laurel Farrer, "Remote Reservations: Why Managers Are Afraid to Let Employees Work Virtually," *Forbes*, February 28, 2019, https://www.forbes.com/sites/laurelfarrer/2019/02/28/ remote-reservations-why-managers-are-afraid-to-let-employees-work-virtually/.

Changes to Employee Productivity

38%	**52%**	**25%**
of respondents said they saw an increase in employee productivity with no notable impact or disruption to the quality of work	of respondents said that the quality of work stayed the same over the 2020 - 2021 period	of respondents said they saw an increase in the quality of work over the 2020 - 2021 period

Source: Fuel50, Global Talent Mobility Best Practice Research

The Return-to-Work Debate Continues to Intensify

Our research found that over three-quarters (76%) of respondents said they would implement a "hybrid working" environment, allowing employees to work from home and the office. However, only 37% of respondents said they would offer this to "all employees," with half (54%) of respondents saying they would only offer hybrid working to "some employees."

Of course, some roles and industries are unable to offer remote working practices. As McKinsey Global Institute highlights, "More than half the workforce, however, has little or no opportunity for remote work. Some of their jobs require collaborating with others or using specialized machinery; other jobs, such as conducting CT scans, must be done on location; and some, such as making deliveries, are performed while out and about."[21]

---

21   Susan Lund, Anu Madgavkar, James Manyika, and Sven Smit, "The Future of Remote Work: An Analysis of 2,000 Tasks, 800 Jobs, and 9 Countries," McKinsey & Company, November 23, 2020, https://www.mckinsey.com/featured-insights/future-of-work/whats-next-for-remote-work-an-analysis-of-2000-tasks-800-jobs-and-nine-countries.

But overall, organizations across the globe are receiving strong resistance from employees when asked to come back into the office full time. As *Forbes* highlights, Apple employees launched a campaign against the company's plan to return to the office.[22] Similarly, the findings of a study of over 10,000 office workers, released by identity firm Okta and Censuswide in June 2021, found that 79% of UK workers want laws to stop them from being forced back into the office.[23] And although office workers outside of the UK did not express the same sentiment around introducing such laws, it is clear employees globally want the freedom to work on their terms, whether that means returning to the office, working remotely, or a mix of both.

Organizations should not resist hybrid work. Research has shown organizations that promote and have embedded flexible working practices benefit from reduced absenteeism, attracting and retaining top talent, improved diversity and inclusion, and increased job satisfaction, energy, and creativity.[24]

---

22 Enrique Dans, "Back to the Office? No Thanks, Say Apple Employees," *Forbes*, June 7, 2021, https://www.forbes.com/sites/enriquedans/2021/06/07/back-to-the-office-nothanks/.

23 Yessi Bello-Perez, "79% of UK Workers Want Laws to Stop Them Being Forced Back into the Office," UNLEASH, June 3, 2021, https://www.unleash.ai/79-of-uk-workers-want-laws-to-stop-them-being-forced-back-into-the-office/.

24 Roy Maurer, "Flexible Work Critical to Retention, Survey Finds," SHRM, September 10, 2019, https://www.shrm.org/resourcesandtools/hr-topics/talent-acquisition/pages/flexible-work-critical-retention.aspx.

The Introduction of Hybrid Working

| 76% of respondents said they would implement a 'hybrid working' environment, allowing employees to work from home and the office | 37% of respondents said they would offer 'hybrid working' to 'all employees' | 54% of respondents said they would offer 'hybrid working' to 'some employees' |

Source: Fuel50, Global Talent Mobility Best Practice Research

KEY FINDING 3: PRODUCTIVITY GAINS ARE AT THE COST OF EMPLOYEE WELL-BEING

From a business perspective, it is good that many organizations experienced increased employee productivity with no noticeable impact on work quality. However, our research suggests this productivity did come at a cost.

Nearly half (47%) of all respondents said that their employee well-being decreased during the pandemic. This finding is hardly surprising when we consider the stressful environmental factors faced by employees globally. There has been considerable uncertainty around job security, fear surrounding health concerns, social isolation, economic instability, and other related factors.

Well-being is becoming a huge focus and concern for organizations everywhere. An article published by *STAT* states that we should be "anticipating a long-term impact on people's mental health…. Experts have also highlighted increases in sleeping problems and alcohol and other substance misuse, and point to clear causes: Uncertainty and fear about the coronavirus itself; job loss and housing and food insecurity; juggling working from home while dealing with cooped-up kids; grief and a loss of social cohesion as a result of restrictions."[25]

A global *Harvard Business Review* study found that 89% of workers said their work life was getting worse, 85% said that their well-being declined, and 56% said that their job demands had increased.[26]

The State of Employee Well-being

Nearly half (47%) of all respondents said that their employee well-being decreased during the pandemic

Source: Fuel50, Global Talent Mobility Best Practice Research

A New Push for Fairness, Inclusivity, and Transparency

In parallel to the seismic shifts caused by COVID-19, we have seen a big shift in the power of the people's voice. During the pandemic, we saw the world stand up and unite in the fight against police brutality

---

25 Andrew Joseph, "Experts Brace for a Long-Term Impact on Mental Health after the Pandemic," *STAT* (blog), May 7, 2021, https://www.statnews.com/2021/05/07/as-the-covid-19-crisis-ebbs-in-the-u-s-experts-brace-for-a-long-term-impact-on-mental-health/.

26 Erica Volini, Jeff Schwartz, Kraig Eaton, David Mallon, Yves Van Durme, Maren Hauptmann, Nic Scoble-Williams, and Shannon Poynton, "The Worker-Employer Relationship Disrupted," Deloitte Insights, July 21, 2021, https://www2.deloitte.com/us/en/insights/focus/human-capital-trends/2021/the-evolving-employer-employee-relationship.html.

and racism. The flare-up of racial tensions in the US and around the world, although unrelated to the pandemic, is equally important in terms of the workplace.

Today, organizations must be truly fair, inclusive, and transparent or risk backlash not only from employees but from customers and investors. In the last five years, organizations have had to up their game. There has always been a movement for more transparency and inclusivity, but it has become more urgent.

> **Today, organizations must be truly fair, inclusive, and transparent or risk backlash not only from employees but from customers and investors.**

This urgency started with the #MeToo movement, as we saw high-profile executives held accountable for sexual harassment and gender discrimination in their organizations. For example, in 2017, after complaints of sexual harassment and discrimination, investors forced the CEO of Uber to resign.[27] And in 2019, the CEO of Nike stepped down after a number of scandals within the company—including women within the organization describing a toxic environment of sexual harassment and gender discrimination.[28]

I asked my team if they had any thoughts to volunteer on the need for change in people practices, based on what they were observing or seeing from their customers. Roel Deuss, a Fuel50 employee in Cali-

---

27   Kate Conger, "Uber Founder Travis Kalanick Leaves Board, Severing Last Tie," *New York Times*, December 24, 2019, sec. Technology, https://www.nytimes.com/2019/12/24/technology/uber-travis-kalanick.html.

28   Julie Creswell and Matthew Futterman, "Nike's Chief Executive, Mark Parker, Is Stepping Down," *New York Times*, October 22, 2019, sec. Business, https://www.nytimes.com/2019/10/22/business/nike-ceo-mark-parker.html.

fornia, writes about the work his partner is doing on the importance of transparency when it comes to gender—and racial—discrimination:

My partner (Katie Carlin) has teamed up with a friend and fellow lawyer to counsel "women in tech" clients. They are seeing women fight to retain their equity shares in the face of discriminatory attempts to force their exits, resulting in hundreds of thousands of dollars in unvested equity left behind. Some of these women are pregnant, some have young children at home. All had great performance reviews prior to the pandemic.

Women in tech lost more than $10.5 billion in equity last year. Katie looked at the data (from Carta, a cap table management software platform used by VC-backed tech companies) on a hunch that her clients' experiences might be representative of a pattern, and there it was: in 2020 women in tech got 47¢ of equity in their startups for every dollar that male employees held. But as bad as that is, it is down from 49¢ to the dollar that we held in 2019.

No one is writing about this. We see lots of talk about making salaries equal, but the real money made in tech is in equity at early-stage companies, and there is very little appreciation for how profoundly unequal the compensation is there. For women and minorities, there is no way of knowing if the offer is fair, and we know from the data that it usually isn't. And then there is the trick of holding on to it in a biased professional environment.

The $10.5 billion loss of the equity pie for women in 2020 is evidence that the stories she's hearing are part of a larger problem that needs to be called out and named. She uses the term "equity heist" for the piece she's been working on. It comes from a conversation she had with a pregnant client who wanted to know about collecting unemployment.

When Katie dug a little deeper, she learned that her company was slated to have the biggest IPO of 2021. At stake was a huge pool of her unvested stock. Fortunately, she was able to help her hold on to it. To do that, though, Katie had to convince her to see it the way that she saw it: "This isn't a termination," Katie told her. "This is a heist." She fought back and they backed down.

While issues of gender discrimination continue, over the course of the pandemic we also saw the Black Lives Matter movement gain new momentum in the protests ignited by the murder of George Floyd. This movement is a reminder to organizations that all employees, irrespective of who they are or where they come from, must be treated equally. We are at a point in history where the world is united against the mistreatment of people in our communities based on the color of their skin—or anything else, for that matter. The world of work needs to respond quickly to ensure all people feel included and are treated equally and fairly. We anticipate that organizations' processes and policies will be subjected to scrutiny to guarantee this. And if that equality and fairness is not achieved, organizations may be affected by "employee walkouts."

The Future of Work Is Here Now

Any revolution needs to harness what the voice of the people is saying. Employee voice surveys are demanding a more democratic employee experience where all employees have visibility to opportunities across the business. As we emerge from the pandemic, we cannot ignore the lessons we have

As we emerge from the pandemic, we cannot ignore the lessons we have learned—because employees are not going to relinquish the newfound power of their voices.

learned—because employees are not going to relinquish the newfound power of their voices. As John Hollon, a Fuel50 employee, writes,

If you are currently employed by a traditional organization and they are in the throes of back to the office, back to before, then this may cause you to reflect on whether or not this is really what you want after two years of blended work-life. The postpandemic intersection with the fourth industrial revolution means the future of work is here now, and it will look different again in the future.

What does the current future of work look like? That's something Fuel50 explored in our 2021 Global Talent Mobility Benchmarking Study, which we will look at in the next chapter.

CUSTOMER JOURNEYS THROUGH CHANGE

Case Study B

> **Organization: A disruptive marketplace technology company that is a household name, employing 23,000 people around the globe and utilizing the services of nearly a million contractors, delivering services to 900 cities around the world.**

Our vision for the talent marketplace is to provide a one-stop personalized experience to employees that empowers them to drive their professional growth to maximize potential toward individual/business success. A desire for us to tap into our current talent portfolio to engage people in high-impact business projects and employees' desire for meaningful development experiences are two of the main drivers for expanding beyond our existing internal transfers into a "talent marketplace" that allows for a variety of projects.

Case Study C

> **Organization: Among the largest global providers of insurance, annuities, and employee benefit programs, with 90 million customers in over 60 countries, employing approximately 50,000 employees globally.**

Our Workforce of the Future Demand Planning and Skills Strategy program: a skills-driven demand-supply ecosystem that will help our businesses identify and build the right people capabilities required to drive our strategic business initiatives. At the same time, the program aims to improve the employee experience by facilitating skills assessment, enabling a talent exchange platform, improving career pathing, and allowing skills-linked learning and development.

As part of this program, we are looking for a technology platform that will deliver a compelling employee experience that centers around helping employees identify their skill gaps and build skills using job opportunities and learning. This platform should link to other parts of the digital ecosystem and enable high adoption across our global employee base.

CHAPTER 3

The Future of Work: What Our Research Is Telling Us

Through her research, Liberty found that there were some common core themes: dissatisfaction, the feeling that it was time for a new ethos, a shift in the vision, values, and operating style of her community. There was a sense that the archaic principles of work distribution were now outdated. Decisions processes were outdated as well. A single patriarchal society in which men made the decisions while women did the work no longer felt optimal. Neither did requiring that people stick to a single task when they may have skills and talents that could contribute to their society in a different way.

A marketplace mentality is what was needed—a place where the whole community could connect and share their individual talents with the wider group.

In 2021, Fuel50 conducted a Global Talent Mobility Benchmarking Study, surveying HR leaders and employees from over 200 organizations across the globe. This Global Talent Mobility Best Practice research was conducted to understand current talent mobility practices, best-in-class talent mobility, and the imperatives for talent mobility in the future across high-performing organizations around the world. The goals of the study were as follows:

- To understand current trends in internal talent mobility and workforce reskilling across the globe

- To learn what best-in-class career growth and talent mobility looks like today

- To ascertain the key imperatives for talent mobility in the coming decade

This chapter will detail some of the key findings from our research study and our extensive analysis of workforce and talent mobility trends.

The Survey Design

The Fuel50 Global Talent Mobility Benchmarking Study explored these topics from two different angles: One section of the survey was designed specifically for HR leaders and contained a mix of 147 multiple-choice and Likert-style questions. The other section was for employees and included 35 questions.

We invited both HR leaders and employees to complete the survey via social media posts and direct email reach-outs to Fuel50's valued community of clients and thought leaders and by asking attendees at our virtual FuelX Conference in April 2021 to respond.

Within the sample of HR leader respondents, the largest proportion worked for organizations within the industries of Professional, Scientific, and Technical Services (25%), followed by Finance & Insurance (9%). Thirty-seven percent of the HR leaders were from organizations with over 10,000 employees. The majority of respondents' organizations had a presence in North America (74%), followed by Europe (44%) and Asia (42%).

HR Leader Respondents: Number of Employees at their Organization

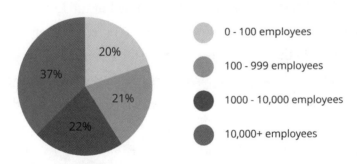

Source: Fuel50, Global Talent Mobility Best Practice Research

HR Leader Respondents: Regions their Organization is Located

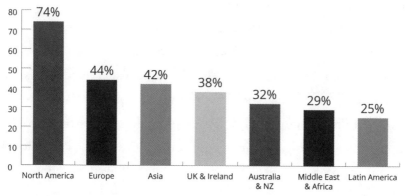

Source: Fuel50, Global Talent Mobility Best Practice Research

Within the sample of employee respondents, 41% have been in paid, full-time employment for over 20 years, with 35% identifying as being in an Individual Contributor/Specialist role and 29% as a Senior Specialist. Most respondents (41%) worked in the industries of Professional, Scientific, and Technical Services. In terms of tenure, 31% have worked in their current organization for 1–2 years. Twenty-two percent have worked at their current organization for 3–5 years.

More than half (53%) of the sample were in North America, with the remainder located in Australasia (Australia and New Zealand) 17%, Europe 11%, Asia 11%, and the rest of the world 9%. The majority of respondents worked in an organization with fewer than 100 employees (39%), with 22% working in organizations with between 110 and 999 employees.

The Future of Work: Strategic Priorities of HR Best-in-Class Organizations versus "the Rest"

Our best-practices research explored how talent mobility experiences differ across high-performing organizations. We categorized high performance in two ways: "Business Performance" and "HR Best in Class."

Business Performance: We identified organizations that had performed in the top 25% of our sample audience who, in the last 12 months, had demonstrated higher revenue growth, total revenue, revenue per employee, percentage of market share, net promoter score, and sales growth year over year. We asked HR leaders to rate how several business metrics have been impacted over the last year (i.e., decreased, stayed the same, increased across revenue growth, revenue per employee, percentage of market share, and sales growth year on year).

The organizations that were classified as top 25% in Business Performance had the following characteristics:

- The majority come from Professional, Scientific, and Technical Service industries (26%)

- The majority are large organizations with 10,000-plus employees (35%)

- The sample includes organizations in North America, Europe, Asia, and the UK

Top "Business Performance" organizations demonstrated:

Higher revenue growth	Higher total revenue	Higher revenue per employee	Higher % of market share	Higher net promoter score	Higher sales growth year-over-year

Source: Fuel50, Global Talent Mobility Best Practice Research

HR Best in Class: Next, we segmented our respondents according to how several HR metrics have been impacted over the last year (i.e., decreased, stayed the same, increased). Based on their responses, we were able to identify organizations that performed in the top 17% of our sample in terms of HR metrics. In the last 12 months, these organizations reported less voluntary attrition, higher internal mobility, lower recruitment costs, fewer unfilled positions, higher employee productivity, and increased spending on training and development.

The best-in-class HR practice group had these characteristics:

- The majority come from the Professional, Scientific, and Technical Service industry (28%)

- The majority are small organizations with fewer than 999 employees (72%)

- The majority of spending is between $500 and $1,000 a year per employee on training and development

- The sample includes organizations in North America, Europe, Asia, and the UK

"HR Best in Class" organizations demonstrated:

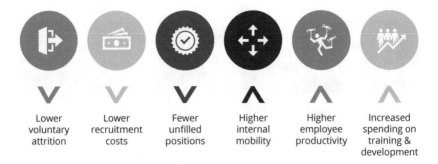

| Lower voluntary attrition | Lower recruitment costs | Fewer unfilled positions | Higher internal mobility | Higher employee productivity | Increased spending on training & development |

Source: Fuel50, Global Talent Mobility Best Practice Research

OUR RESEARCH FOUND A STRONG LINK BETWEEN HR BEST IN CLASS AND BUSINESS PERFORMANCE

Organizations in our sample that ranked as HR Best in Class (i.e., they had lower voluntary attrition, higher internal mobility, lower recruitment costs, fewer unfilled positions, higher employee productivity, increased training, and development spending) also outperformed organizations in Business Performance (i.e., they had higher revenue growth, total revenue, revenue per employee, percentage of market share, net promoter score, sales growth year over year).

This finding provides a compelling reason for organizations to pivot their focus to implementing the tactics and focus areas we will be discussing in this chapter and throughout this book. These tactics and focus areas drive enhanced HR practices—leading to increased business performance.

Why should organizations strive to be "HR Best in Class"?

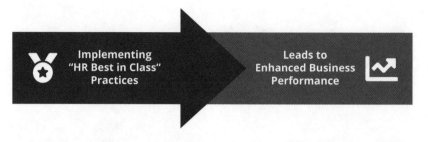

Source: Fuel50, Global Talent Mobility Best Practice Research

The Critical Levers to HR Best in Class

Our research found that those in the HR Best in Class group were investing in some critical levers to drive better performance on HR metrics across three audiences: the organizational lens, the leader lens, and the HR lens. Investing in employee development was strongly correlated with best-in-class organizational performance, as well as enabling leaders to support employee development, while HR departments were enabled to have talent and skills intelligence that gave visibility to bench strength.

What do the HR Best in Class organizations prioritize in their business to enhance their HR practices? These are the key findings from our research:

What do "HR Best in Class" organizations prioritize?

 The organization places strategic importance on employee development (r = .293**)
- Invests adequately in employee development
- Provides development to all its employees

 Leaders take an active role in developing others (r = .252**)
- Leaders identify and fairly distribute a range of learning/development opportunities to members of their teams
- They role model by developing themselves
- They support internal mobility

 HR has visibility to employee talent bench strength (r = .219**)
- HR have tools/technology giving them visibility to employee capability strengths and needs across the organization, allowing them to search for skills and capabilities and build talent pipelines

 Leaders are given tools & resources to support employee development (r = .205**)
- Leaders are upskilled and given resources to help others develop their careers
- Leaders have tools/technology giving them visibility to employee capability strengths and needs across the organization, allowing them to search for skills and capabilities and build talent pipelines autonomously from HR

Source: Fuel50, Global Talent Mobility Best Practice Research

The Critical Levers to "HR Best in Class"

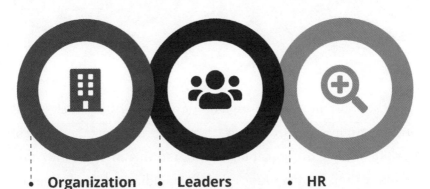

Organization
- Invests adequately in employee development (r=.264**)
- Provides development to all its employees (r=.273**)

Leaders
- Identify appropriate ways to address the developmental needs of their team (r=.301**)
- Are recognized and/or rewarded for developing their team members (r=.335**)

HR
- Have visibility to the talent bench strength (i.e., capability strengths & needs across the organization) (r=.282**)

Source: Fuel50, Global Talent Mobility Best Practice Research

The Top Strategic HR Priorities

With the world of work evolving so rapidly, we wanted to explore what strategic HR priorities and business practices organizations are focusing on now and what they intend to focus on for the future.

We asked HR leaders across the globe what their top strategic HR priorities are for the next two years. What we found was that HR Best in Class organizations are prioritizing the future of work, whereas for the rest of organizations, the future of work didn't even make it into the top five.

What are the top strategic HR priorities for your organization?

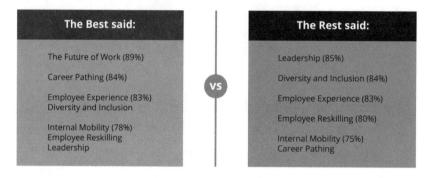

The Best said:		The Rest said:
The Future of Work (89%)		Leadership (85%)
Career Pathing (84%)	VS	Diversity and Inclusion (84%)
Employee Experience (83%) Diversity and Inclusion		Employee Experience (83%)
		Employee Reskilling (80%)
Internal Mobility (78%) Employee Reskilling Leadership		Internal Mobility (75%) Career Pathing

Source: Fuel50, Global Talent Mobility Best Practice Research

The most progressive organizations in the best-in-class HR practice group (i.e., HR Best in Class) are prioritizing the future of work (89%) and career pathing (84%), showing more prioritization on future thinking and future capability building; while all organizations equally prioritized employee experience (83%), diversity and inclusion (83%), and internal mobility, employee reskilling and skill building, and leadership (78%).

Top Findings on the Future of Work

The global pandemic has driven significant acceleration to the future of work, with the overnight pivot to remote work and people leveraging technology in new and innovative ways. As we shift toward an increasingly digital standard, the preferences and expectations of employees are dramatically changing. For organizations to build successful environments for their workers, more progressive strategies must be implemented. As Gartner states, "Leaders need to consider the predictions for what the future of work will look like and assess the likelihood of each trend impacting the organization."[29]

Those organizations that prioritize the future of work will be best prepared and ready to respond to whatever the future may bring.

Those organizations that prioritize the future of work will be best prepared and ready to respond to whatever the future may bring. Here are three key findings on the future of work that emerged from our research:

---

29   Mary Baker, "Future of Work Tops HR Priorities for 2020–21," Gartner, July 6, 2020, https://www.gartner.com/smarterwithgartner/future-of-work-tops-hr-priorities-for-2020-21.

AGILE SKILLS AND PROJECT-BASED WORKFORCES ARE HERE TO STAY

A few years ago, McKinsey observed that the agile organization was becoming the new organizational paradigm.[30] Fast-forward to today, and we now know that not only was that prediction spot on but that building an agile workforce has become critically important for any organization looking to grow and be highly successful for today and tomorrow.

Skills-based organizations have a more agile and employee-centric approach to work where employees are valued for their skills rather than their job title, level, or educational qualifications. It is a new operating model of work where employees are matched to tasks and projects based on skills, capabilities, and interests.[31] Focusing on skill sets instead of job experience can help organizations optimize their existing talent pool. Skills-based organizations are moving away from traditional job structures and adopting agile talent development strategies. They have flatter, team-based structures with leaner job architectures (i.e., fewer levels and job titles as well as broader pay structures).[32] In our *Fuel50 Capability Trends Report*, we explored the likelihood of organizations transitioning from being job based to skills based. In the event of this, we suggest critical organizational, leader-

30 Wouter Aghina, Karin Ahlback, Aaron De Smet, Gerald Lackey, Michael Lurie, Monica Murarka, and Christopher Handscomb, "The Five Trademarks of Agile Organizations," McKinsey & Company, January 22, 2018, https://www.mckinsey.com/business-functions/people-and-organizational-performance/our-insights/the-five-trademarks-of-agile-organizations.

31 Michael Griffiths, "The Skills-Based Organization: Fueling the 21st Century Enterprise with Skills," Deloitte, September 14, 2021, http://www2.deloitte.com/us/en/blog/human-capital-blog/2021/skills-based-talent-strategies.html.

32 "The Organization of the Future: The Right Job Architecture Can Drive Your Transformation," Deloitte, 2017, https://www2.deloitte.com/us/en/pages/human-capital/articles/job-architecture-of-the-future.html.

ship, and employee capabilities to support this transformation to help harness the latest global capability trends to ensure that your organizational talent strategy is aligned to the current driving global forces.

Agility and resilience in the workforce are in hot demand right now. People are pivoting, upskilling, and being redeployed into different parts of the business, so having an agile workforce that is skill ready enough to be reassigned internally is something of incredible economic value.

An evolving trend emerged from our research, with close to 70% of respondents using project work for employee development. As defined by *Forbes*, project-based work has clear goals, milestones, and deliverables, with defined start and end dates. Projects or gigs may take hours, months, or longer, with the work aligned to business needs and objectives, not specific roles. And the individuals brought together to work on projects could be permanent employees or freelancers.[33]

The feedback loop that takes place after a project or gig, for the skills and contributions that that person has made, becomes a kind of virtuous gain cycle. It is a success spiral for the individual and for the business—a learning loop. Therefore, there is the opportunity for employee development and more workforce agility as there are more people ready, skilled, and able to support with rapidly changing business demands.

Over 50% of our respondents said they currently have a project-based workforce or intend to implement this way of working within the next 12 months. Organizations that have already implemented agile skills and a project-based workforce cite increased innovation,

33   Yolanda Lau, "Council Post: How Organizations Can Become Project-Based in the Future of Work," *Forbes*, June 2, 2021, https://www.forbes.com/sites/forbeshumanresourcescouncil/2021/06/02/how-organizations-can-become-project-based-in-the-future-of-work/.

speed, and efficiency due to being able to draw on the required skills both internally and externally.

Based on our findings, we are confident that agile skills and project-based workforces are here to stay.

THE BENEFITS OF BEING A SKILLS-BASED ORGANIZATION

Moving away from rigid job architectures to an agile skills-based approach has many organizational and employee benefits. Companies that have clear visibility to all the different types of talent at their disposal, with a line of sight to how work is getting done, by whom, with what skills, performed where and at what value, will have an immediate and significant competitive advantage.

- Increased talent supply: By tapping into skills as opposed to job titles only, organizations can source talent from a broader, more diverse talent pool at scale, which allows them to address talent demand and supply more effectively. In turn, this presents a different way of solving talent shortages. Effective skills-management strategies enable organizations to pivot in response to rapid dynamic and competitive environmental demands. And visibility to the skills pool makes it easier to transfer skills to other parts of the organization affected by change.

- Enhanced career opportunities and growth: An organization that adopts a transparent culture around skills can promote curiosity and creativity by enabling employees to think outside of the box about work experiences and, ultimately, their career trajectories. When organizations appreciate skill sets for their collective value of interdisciplinary and cross-functional knowledge, it opens up more growth opportunities for employees.

- Reduced bias in selection and promotion: Focusing on skills provides a more objective assessment of suitable talent in hiring and promotion processes and may also reduce unconscious biases associated with these processes.

Organizations are shifting to agile skills and project-based work

Over 50% of respondents said they either do this now or will implement this way of working within the next 12 months.

Close to 70% of respondents are using project-based work for the purpose of employee development.

Source: Fuel50, Global Talent Mobility Best Practice Research

HOLACRACY MAY BE THE FUTURE, BUT MOST ARE NOT READY TO RELINQUISH JOB TITLES JUST YET

Job titles have been a hot topic of discussion over the years. It is fair to say that many people advocate for job titles, as they effectively communicate the type of work someone does and their level of experience.[34] As quoted by *Harvard Business Review*, "your job title can have a big impact on your day-to-day happiness and engagement," says Dan Cable, professor at London Business School. "It is a form of self-expression in the workplace," he says. "It is a symbolic representa-

---

34   Biron Clark, "Are Job Titles Important? (This Might Surprise You)," Career Sidekick, November 12, 2019, https://careersidekick.com/are-job-titles-important/.

tion of what you do and the value that you bring."[35] But equally, job titles can be vague, meaningless, and inconsistent from organization to organization. According to *Fast Company*, Pearl Meyer data found that nearly 30% of firms have job-titling practices that can vary from one department to another.[36]

Several futurists have predicted that organizations will relinquish job titles altogether, opting for employees to be recognized simply by the skills, capabilities, and experiences they possess. In their view, employees will move from project to project rather than being restricted to a specific role or job title.

We can also look to progressive organizations such as Gore-Tex, Patagonia, and Zappos, who are championing completely flat organizational structures and a way of working that does not require restrictive job titles. As Tony Hsieh, CEO of Zappos, explained,

> Research shows that every time the size of a city doubles innovation or productivity per resident increases by 15 percent. But when companies get bigger, innovation or productivity per employee generally goes down. So, we're trying to figure out how to structure Zappos more like a city, and less like a bureaucratic corporation. In a city, people and businesses are self-organizing. We're trying to do the same thing by switching from a normal hierarchical structure to

35 Rebecca Knight, "How to Ask for the Job Title You Deserve," *Harvard Business Review*, July 17, 2017, https://hbr.org/2017/07/how-to-ask-for-the-job-title-you-deserve.

36 Gwen Moran, "Why Your Job Title Means a Lot More Than You Think," *Fast Company*, September 9, 2014, https://www.fastcompany.com/3035359/why-your-job-title-means-a-lot-more-than-you-think.

a system called Holacracy, which enables employees to act more like entrepreneurs.[37]

However, this vision is not supported by our research. Sixty-four percent of respondents said they have no intention of moving to a "job title–less" workforce. This suggests that job titles are here to stay for now, and while organizations will move to more project-based work, people will continue to play specific roles within the project teams they are members of (i.e., analyst, project manager, online marketer).

The Future of Work: To Title or Not To Title

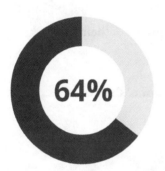

64% of respondents said they have no intention of moving to a 'job title-less' workforce.

Source: Fuel50, Global Talent Mobility Best Practice Research

TALENT POOLS ARE CHANGING SHAPE

Our research has revealed that many organizations are now seeking to move to a broader view of their talent—what we call "Horizon Talent Pools." Horizon Talent Pools emerge when an organization utilizes the skills and capabilities of both its internal talent pool and a contingent workforce (i.e., part-time employees, contractors, prospective employees, and gig workers). But for organizations to mine the skills

---

37 "Zappos.Com Careers," accessed November 8, 2021, https://jobs.jobvite.com/zappos/p/how.

internally and externally, they need technology to enable visibility to their talent bench strength.

We found that 55% of organizations currently utilize a contingent workforce to draw on part-time employees, contractors, and gig workers to source the skills they need. However, only 30% of respondents have visibility to their talent bench strength across both internal and external populations.

Our prediction is that acquiring technology to enhance talent visibility will be a strategic priority for organizations over the next 24 months to ensure that they can effectively leverage the capabilities and skills available to them. This prediction is supported by our finding that one in four respondents intend to increase their scope of visibility to talent within the next 12 months.

Organizations are seeking a broader view of their talent

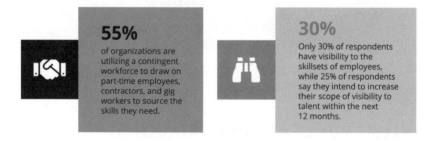

Source: Fuel50, Global Talent Mobility Best Practice Research

TALENT VISIBILITY IS A CRUCIAL COMPONENT

Despite over 75% of organizations having strategic HR priorities aimed at understanding, building, and mobilizing their talent, less than half of HR leaders had visibility to the skills and capabilities within their organization.

HR Leaders' strategic organizational priorities for the next 2 years

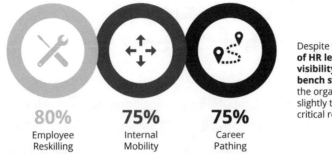

80%
Employee
Reskilling

75%
Internal
Mobility

75%
Career
Pathing

Despite this, **only 43% of HR leaders have visibility to their talent bench strength** across the organization (rising slightly to 47% for critical roles).

Source: Fuel50, Global Talent Mobility Best Practice Research

If organizations were to give HR leaders visibility to their employees' capabilities and skills, they could start to unlock the full potential of their workforce and do incredible things. Too often there is an unrealistic expectation that HR and business leaders should be able to drive positive change in an organization without critical information on the talents, skills, and experience that already exists in their employee population.

Revealing the hidden talent in any organization requires transparency as to the skills and capabilities that people currently possess, as well as those that they are willing to grow and develop. However, 39% of HR leaders said their HR teams do not have access to tools to help them search for skills and capabilities across the organization to build talent pipelines.

What Do We Know about Organizations with High Visibility to Their Talent?

Those organizations and HR teams that had high visibility to their talent bench strength (i.e., capability strengths and needs), with tools to help them search for skills and capabilities across the organization to help build talent pipelines, were more likely to fill positions internally and have better diversity practices.

Benefits of High Visibility to Talent Bench Strength

More Positions Filled Internally
r = .304**

• Have well-embedded and effective internal recruitment practices
• Ability to source and fill roles internally
• Reduced recruitment costs
• Increased time to productivity
• Increased talent retention

Talent Visibility Across the Business

Better Diversity Practices
r = .242**

• Prioritize diversity & inclusion
• Enabled to actively promote diversity at all levels
• Identify and retain diverse talent
• Focus on D&I as their strategic goals and set diversity-related recruitment goals
• Report publicly on D&I people metrics

Source: Fuel50, Global Talent Mobility Best Practice Research

MORE POSITIONS FILLED INTERNALLY

Organizations with high visibility to their talent were more likely to have well-embedded and effective internal recruitment practices. This gives them the ability to find and fill roles internally rather than relying heavily on external recruitment practices.

Providing visibility to employees' capabilities and skills also gives HR leaders and teams the ability to approach employees about open positions. The benefits of this include reduced recruitment costs and increased time to productivity while increasing talent retention and engagement.

BETTER DIVERSITY PRACTICES

Organizations with high visibility to their talent were more likely to prioritize and promote diversity and inclusion. More specifically, they were enabled to actively promote diversity at all levels of the organizational hierarchy. They were also able to identify and actively retain diverse talent, focus on diversity and inclusion practices as a strategic goal, and set diversity-related recruitment goals. As a result of this, they were then able to report publicly on their diversity and inclusion people metrics.

WHAT BUSINESS OUTCOMES DID ORGANIZATIONS SEE FROM GIVING HR INCREASED TALENT VISIBILITY?

Our research found that those organizations with HR teams that had visibility to talent across their organization, possessing tools and technology to help them build talent pipelines, were more likely to have the following:

- Lower voluntary attrition

- Lower recruitment costs

- Lower unfilled positions

- Higher internal mobility

- Higher employee productivity

- Higher training and development spend

Best-in-class organizations are investing more in training and development to achieve these gains.

Business Outcomes from Giving HR Increased Talent Visibility

Higher internal mobility

Higher employee productivity

Higher training and development spending

Talent Visibility Across the Business

Lower voluntary attrition

Lower recruitment costs

Fewer unfilled positions

Source: Fuel50, Global Talent Mobility Best Practice Research

As mentioned, our findings show that HR leaders have the desire to expand their visibility to talent to include both internal and external employee skills and capabilities. However, less than 33% of organizations currently have the technology to see their talent, and only 25% want to acquire technology to enable this visibility within the next 12 months.

This shifted again in 2022 when we saw a dramatic increase in some organizations's desires to have talent visibility through a talent marketplace. The Fuel50 2022 Talent Technology Marketplace study showed us that two out of three enterprise organizations wanted better skills intelligence in their organization.

HOW CAN ORGANIZATIONS INCREASE THEIR LEVELS OF TALENT VISIBILITY?

Future-ready organizations are leveraging technology—like AI—to create talent marketplaces that focus on employee connectivity and make a significant impact in the transformation of a workplace. This technology really helps open doors for not only employees but the

HR teams who are tasked with recruiting and retaining the best teams possible.

With AI, companies can determine where to redeploy people based on their core talents and interests, or by identifying projects that employees might be interested in across the entire organization. Overall, this puts the power into the hands of employees (both internal and external) and allows them to have more access to open job and project opportunities, as well as increases their ability to connect with potential mentors, career paths, and necessary tools to grow future skills.

INVESTING IN TALENT MOBILITY

Results show that the best in class career pathing and development practices are connected to improved HR functions and better business performance at large. A closer drill down into these relationships shows that best career engagement practices lead to business return primarily by building internal talent bench strength. Top performing organizations built a broad and diversified internal talent pool, which provided them with sufficient internal talent to address strategic challenges.

Buying talent from outside will, on average, not only cost at least 18% more, but outside hires take three years to perform as well as internal hires in the same job. According to The Best Practice Institute, the outsiders brought in had worse performance reviews during their first two years on the job. An external hire is 61% more likely to be fired, they take twice as long to get up to speed, and SHRM Research clearly shows that promotions from within have a much higher probability of success than hiring from the outside. The superiority of internal promotions over external hires increases at the highest levels of the organization, even though there is a natural tendency to believe external hires are usually superior.

Leveraging Fuel50 Career Engagement Benchmark Practices, they were able to correlate overall revenue growth and revenue growth per employee with improvement on a range of key HR performance metrics including reduced attrition, reduced absenteeism, and lower overall recruiting costs (r =.421**).

Fuel50 Career Engagement Benchmarking Study, March 2019 Edition

The Future of Work Belongs to the Flexible, Agile, and Resilient

Ultimately, HR teams and leaders have an important role to play in this new world of work. As David Perring, director of research at Fosway Group, highlights, "Organizations achieve through their people. So, the opportunity to create higher-performing organizations is really at HR's fingertips—if we choose to harness it."[38]

---

38   David Perring, "Does Your Organization Have a Future without Talent Mobility?" *Fuel50* (blog), September 11, 2020, https://www.fuel50.com/2020/09/does-your-organization-have-a-future-without-talent-mobility/.

But despite what many futurists and analysts are saying, most organizations are not ready for the future of work yet.

Most Organizations are Not Ready for the Future of Work

32.1%	24.5%	64.2%
said they utilize a contingent workforce for their skills needs now and intend to continue	said they will opt for a more agile skills project-based workforce in the next 12 months	said they have no intention of removing job titles and moving to project-based work
42.5%	24.5%	25.5%
said they use project work (gigs) for the purpose of employee development now and intend to continue	said they want visibility to skills inside and outside the organization in the next 12 months	said they have no intention of moving to a simplified, flat organizational structure

Source: Fuel50, Global Talent Mobility Best Practice Research

People practices, business practices, and strategic HR priorities will need to be better than they were last decade. More human centric, intelligent, more robust in their skills and capability matching, more learning and growth-oriented, more enabling, and better able to deliver the talent optimization that organizations will need in the coming decade.

For organizations and HR leaders striving to be best in class, talent intelligence and talent decision-making right now are critical. Companies should ensure they have critical talent where they need it most and a talent supply to support that. That visibility to talent intelligence is gold dust for any organization.

Smart, forward-thinking organizations will focus on prioritizing this demand for talent visibility and will work to implement a new set of norms that both enable and encourage internal mobility. There needs to be a deep systemic organizational commitment, investment, and passion for the growth of people and their skills, and within that, a commitment to harness internal mobility as a lever for building skills and growing talent. Those that do this will be far more likely to thrive in the future of work.

Internal Recruitment Practices and Internal Talent Mobility

Internal recruitment, career development, and upskilling are all absolutely in demand right now. People are willing to learn more within their current organization and even their current role. People are actively looking to grow and develop and are seeking opportunities to move forward in their careers.

Deloitte explains that "internal mobility is a driver of growth in today's digitally powered, highly competitive global economy." In fact, their survey found that "the fastest-growing organizations (those growing at 10 percent or more compared to the prior year) were twice as likely to have excellent talent mobility programs than organizations that were not growing at all, and more than three times more likely than organizations whose revenues were shrinking."[39]

Not only is internal talent mobility a major source of critical talent, competitive advantage, and a driver of growth; it is also a source of employee engagement. As the *2019 Deloitte Global Human Capital Trends Report* highlights, "Agile organizations and career models dramatically improve employee engagement and commitment."

"To fuel growth," the report continues, "organizations need to more effectively tap their current workforce to identify and deploy people with the required skills, capabilities, motivation, and knowledge

---

39 Indranil Roy, Yves Van Durme, and Maren Hauptmann, "Talent Mobility: Winning the War on the Home Front," Deloitte Insights, April 11, 2019, https://www2.deloitte.com/content/www/us/en/insights/focus/human-capital-trends/2019/internal-talent-mobility.html.

of the organization, its infrastructure, and its culture. Creating better programs to facilitate internal mobility can pay off in multiple areas: growth, employee engagement, and business performance."[40]

As Josh Bersin puts it, internal mobility is now mission critical.[41]

It is also important to note, as Deloitte does, that "an internal hire need not be a 'perfect' fit for a role to be afforded an opportunity for growth or skills development."[42] Investing in your people and their future careers within the organization is highly likely to boost employee engagement.

As explained in our November 2020 Best Practice Guide to Internal Talent Mobility, "Driven employees want transparency into opportunities to learn new skills, take on different assignments, shadow on projects, find mentors and volunteer opportunities, and work with different teams and managers—looking internally for personal growth journeys and new challenges."[43]

Here is what we know about why internal talent mobility is high on the agenda for organizations everywhere. Fifty-five percent of employees said they are likely to look for a new job in the next 12 months, with social networks being the number one source of hires,

40 *Human Capital Trends Report 2019*, Deloitte, 2019, https://www2.deloitte.com/ro/en/pages/human-capital/articles/2019-deloitte-global-human-capital-trends.html.

41 Josh Bersin, "Career Management Goes Mission Critical: And It's All about to Change," Josh Bersin, June 18, 2019, https://joshbersin.com/2019/06/career-management-goes-mission-critical-and-its-all-about-to-change/.

42 Indranil Roy, Yves Van Durme, and Maren Hauptmann, "Accessing Talent: It's More than Acquisition," Deloitte Insights, April 11, 2019, https://www2.deloitte.com/content/www/us/en/insights/focus/human-capital-trends/2019/talent-acquisition-trends-strategies.html.

43 Fuel50, "Best Practice Guide to Internal Talent Mobility Playbook," accessed November 8, 2021, https://www.fuel50.com/resources/best-practice-guide-to-internal-talent-mobility/.

followed by job boards. [44] And only 29% of HR leaders said employees were exploring career paths internally. [45]

Fifty percent of employees said it is easier to find a new job outside their organization than inside. Plus, less than 33% of organizations have the technology to see their talent, despite over 75% having strategic priorities to improve their internal talent mobility initiatives.

Why Organizations Need Internal Talent Mobility Right Now

50% of employees said it's easier to find a new job outside their organization than inside.

55% of employees said they are likely to look for a new job in the next 12 months.

Less than 33% of organizations have the technology to see their talent.

Social networks are the #1 source of hires followed by job boards.

Only 29% of HR leaders said employees had the tools to explore career paths internally.

Over 75% of organizations have strategic priorities to improve internal mobility.

Source: Fuel50, Global Talent Mobility Best Practice Research

The business benefits of internal recruitment and talent mobility are incredible. Internal hires cost half as much, take half the time to onboard, and are typically promoted faster. Plus they have increased engagement and productivity and are far less likely to leave. On the other hand, external hires are 61% more likely to be fired, are paid up to 20% more, and take almost two times longer to onboard—not

44   Sarah Foster, "Survey: 55% Expecting to Search for a New Job over the Next 12 Months," Bankrate, August 23, 2021, https://www.bankrate.com/personal-finance/job-seekers-survey-august-2021/.

45   "The Ultimate List of Hiring Statistics for Hiring Managers, HR Professionals, and Recruiters," LinkedIn, 2015, https://business.linkedin.com/content/dam/business/talent-solutions/global/en_us/c/pdfs/Ultimate-List-of-Hiring-Stats-v02.04.pdf.

to mention they cost well over two times as much as internal hires to recruit.[46]

The Current State of Talent Mobility and Recruitment Strategy

Our research has confirmed that internal mobility is one of the top strategic HR priorities for all organizations across the globe right now. Sixty percent of respondents said internal talent mobility is extremely important in their organization, with 43% stating that reskilling is a top strategic priority.

Internal Talent Mobility is a Top Strategic Priority for HR

 60% of respondents said internal talent mobility is extremely important in their organization.

 43% of respondents stated that reskilling is a top strategic priority for their organization.

Source: Fuel50, Global Talent Mobility Best Practice Research

However, while respondents *said* that talent mobility is a top strategic priority for their organization, our findings show they don't have the numbers to suggest it is happening across the business. Respondents said that reskilling is a top priority, but they can't quantify how many people have made an internal move.

When the pandemic first hit, it shook the world of work. Business confidence dropped, uncertainty rose, and HR's immediate response

---

46   Jefferson Online, "Hiring Quality Employees: Internal vs External Recruiting," October 10, 2019, https://online.jefferson.edu/human-resources/internal-vs-external-recruiting/.

was to freeze external recruitment until levels of clarity and confidence began to rise again.

With external recruitment on hold, it would be fair to assume this would have created a strong catalyst for recruitment teams to focus their efforts on mining their internal talent to fill critical roles. But our research suggests this wasn't the case, with only 25% of respondents agreeing that they had seen a shift in recruitment ratios with their organization filling roles more via internal recruitment versus external recruitment over the last 18 months.

As we enter this new world of work, and "as organizations globalize and compete aggressively for top talent, the importance of internal, enterprise-wide talent mobility has become paramount," Deloitte writes in their *2019 Human Capital Trends Report*. "Organizations can no longer expect to source and hire enough people with all the capabilities they need; they must move and develop people internally to be able to thrive."[47]

CURRENT RATES OF INTERNAL RECRUITMENT

Our findings indicate there is significant room for improvement when it comes to internal recruitment and internal talent mobility. Fifty-eight percent of respondents said they look internally first when filling open positions, and 35% said most senior leadership roles are filled internally. But actual rates of internal movement across all organizations are still surprisingly low.

A third said their overall internal hires are less than 25% compared to external recruitment, and 22% said that less than 5% of their people participated in a lateral move last year.

---

47   *Human Capital Trends Report 2019*, Deloitte, 2019, https://www2.deloitte.com/ro/en/pages/human-capital/articles/2019-deloitte-global-human-capital-trends.html.

Even more surprising is that 35% of respondents said they do not know their internal recruitment ratio. A quarter of respondents said they do not know what range internal hires sit within in their organization, and 50% of organizations do not track the impact of talent mobility practices against objective criteria. As a result, internal recruitment and internal talent mobility metrics are not captured or reported.

This discovery led us to question what is stopping organizations from having well-embedded internal recruitment practices. Why are organizations still relying so heavily on external recruitment, particularly when they already have people internally who can fill the role with their current skills or grow into the role with minimal training and development?

What is Stopping Organizations from Achieving Internal Mobility?

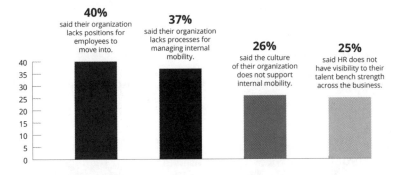

Source: Fuel50, Global Talent Mobility Best Practice Research

WHAT ARE THE TOP BLOCKERS TO INTERNAL MOBILITY? AND HOW CAN THEY BE SOLVED?

With 50% of employee respondents saying it is easier to find a role outside of their organization than inside, there is a pressing need for organizations to review and improve their internal recruitment practices. And, particularly as we now face "the Great Resignation," internal talent mobility is a valuable tool to support talent retention.

Employees leave organizations when they do not see a developmental path, and they go to organizations where they can see a clear future.[48] People want visibility to internal opportunities for career development, and many are ready and willing to jump ship to gain it.

Here are four of the top blockers to internal mobility, as highlighted by our research, and some actionable suggestions for how to overcome them:

1. An Organizational Culture That Doesn't Encourage Internal Mobility

Twenty-two percent of respondents said that lateral moves are not encouraged in their organization. When exploring how organization size affected responses, 38% of organizations with more than 10,000 employees stated the culture of their organization does not support internal mobility, versus 18–21% of organizations of varying sizes below 10,000 employees.

One factor that could be contributing to this block to internal mobility is talent hoarding by leaders and managers. As Gallup explains,

> The problem may be with your managers. Your managers— knowingly or unknowingly—may be hoarding your top talent. As a result, they may be inadvertently sending your best people to your competition.... Managers should be advocates for their employees. They should help personalize roles and career paths in a way that makes sense with an individual's dreams, strengths, and priorities. Like a coach who

---

48 Ed O'Boyle and Ryan Pendell, "How to Stop Your Managers from Talent Hoarding," Gallup.com, August 13, 2019, https://www.gallup.com/workplace/263558/stop-managers-talent-hoarding.aspx.

always thinks about the next game, managers should direct conversations toward future performance and its rewards.[49]

Lateral Moves are Not Encouraged

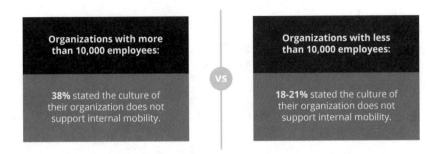

Source: Fuel50, Global Talent Mobility Best Practice Research

Possible solution: An effective tactic for creating an organizational culture of internal mobility is to reward and recognize leaders and managers for supporting internal mobility statistics (i.e., the number of team members they develop that then move on to other areas of the business) or for attracting talent into their team from across the organization (i.e., talent agents).

As Larry McAlister, then VP of Global Talent at NetApp, told us when we asked his views on talent mobility, "[Managers] should be a net exporter of talent. That's a great goal to spread your influence around the organization with people that you have managed who are now in different areas of the business."

There are some habits that leaders can develop to become true talent agents. As *Harvard Business Review* outlines,

Talent is the make-or-break issue for business success. Few great entrepreneurs and CEOs of our acquaintance would

---

49   Ibid.

contest that statement. If you are a leader who's serious about improving your capacity to attract the best talent, you need to develop the habits of a true talent magnet.... Our recommendation: cultivate the best talent you can, and keep these individuals apprised of your work, purpose, and ongoing mission. Let them know who you are as a person. Best talents have lots of options. Don't be surprised when they say "no" to you. Never give up. Keep coming back over a number of years and when these talents are finally ready to move and know how you are different, they will come to you.[50]

2. A Lack of Positions for Employees to Move Into

Forty percent of respondents stated that their organization lacks positions for employees to move into. When exploring how organization size affected responses, 52% of organizations with fewer than 100 employees said they lack roles for people to move into, versus 30% of organizations with over 10,000 employees. This finding is intuitive, as we would anticipate smaller organizations to be leaner in roles and opportunities.

Often when an organization lacks positions for employees to move into, there is either little awareness and marketing of new roles and opportunities across the organization, or employees are not frequently directed to or reminded of internal job boards (if they exist at all). If internal job boards exist, they are old, outdated, and not user friendly or engaging, turning employees off.

---

50 Anthony K. Tjan, "The Six Habits of a Talent Magnet," *Harvard Business Review,* January 24, 2011, https://hbr.org/2011/01/the-six-habits-of-a-talent-mag.

Not Enough Open Roles to Support Employee Mobility

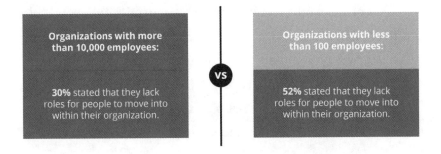

Source: Fuel50, Global Talent Mobility Best Practice Research

Possible solution: If organizations don't have open vacancies, it is still critical to offer employees opportunities to develop their skills. Gigs and stretch assignments are exceptional tools for boosting talent retention in the absence of open positions. And project-based work gives employees the opportunity to learn and grow while the business harnesses the internal skills and talents they already have.

As discovered by our research on career agility, 86% of employees think they have skills and talents today that are not being used by their organization.[51] Companies need to create transparency to be able to join the dots between the untapped skills and talents that employees have and that the organization needs.

This is where technology can make a huge difference. For example, Fuel50's Gigs functionality gives employees access to career growth and stretch assignments. Leaders across the business can post a gig, promote it, review and assign applicants, and follow up with feedback to support organization-wide career development and talent

---

51   "Career Agility & Engagement White Paper," Fuel50, accessed November 8, 2021, https://www.fuel50.com/resources/career-agility-engagement/.

harnessing. Gigs are suggested to employees based on their skills and talents they wish to develop, supporting their career growth goals.

One of the world's leading biotech companies, which was also the first to release a COVID-19 test, used Fuel50's Gigs functionality to deliver over one million hours of unlocked productivity. In just six months, one million gig experience hours were taken across the business. As a result, their workforce was ready to pivot and respond to the unprecedented circumstances brought about by the pandemic.

3. Poor Processes for Managing Internal Mobility

Our research found that 37% of all respondents said their organization lacks effective processes for managing internal mobility, and 35% of HR leaders said their employees face challenges moving into new positions when there is an opening and/or learning opportunity.

Not only that, 50% of respondents do not track the impact of talent mobility practices against objective criteria. When exploring how organization size affected responses, 46% of organizations with more than 10,000 employees stated their organization lacks an effective process for managing internal mobility, versus 14% of organizations with fewer than 100 employees.

Organizations Lack Effective Internal Mobility Processes

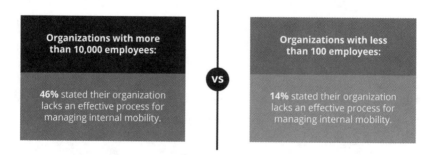

Organizations with more than 10,000 employees:

46% stated their organization lacks an effective process for managing internal mobility.

VS

Organizations with less than 100 employees:

14% stated their organization lacks an effective process for managing internal mobility.

Source: Fuel50, Global Talent Mobility Best Practice Research

Possible solution: Organizations with poor internal mobility processes would benefit from running focus groups with employees to better understand how internal mobility processes could be improved. These focus groups should cover areas such as the following:

- *Access to information:* How easy is it to find information about open roles across the organization? Are employees notified of these, or do they have to find them? Where is this information housed, and how frequently is it updated?

- *Ease of application:* How easy is it to apply for open internal positions? What information is typically requested? How long does the internal recruitment process take?

- *Ideas for process improvements:* How could internal recruitment processes be improved to make them easier and more user friendly?

4. HR Does Not Have Visibility to Talent Bench Strength

A quarter of respondents said their HR teams do not have visibility to the talent bench strength across their organization. When exploring how organization size affected responses, we found that 17% of organizations with between 1,000 and 10,000 employees said that HR does not have visibility to the talent bench strength across their organization, versus 28% of organizations with fewer than 100 employees. Ironically, smaller organizations appear to have less visibility to their internal talent.

As we know, talent visibility is a crucial component to talent mobility and the future of work. And there are clear business benefits to having high visibility to talent bench strength. These include lower voluntary attrition, lower recruitment costs, lower unfilled positions, higher internal mobility, higher employee productivity, and higher training and development spend, as best-in-class organizations invest more in training and development to achieve these gains.

Lack of Visibility to Talent

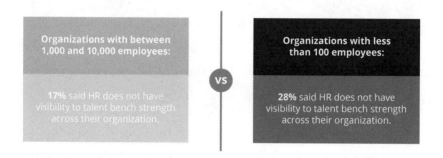

Source: Fuel50, Global Talent Mobility Best Practice Research

Possible solution: In our Best Practice Guide to Internal Talent Mobility, we highlighted that internal recruitment practices and talent mobility are going to be essential in this new era of work and "a talent marketplace solution is required to apply this talent operating model in a sustainable and scalable way."[52]

Today's best-in-class talent marketplaces are aiming to connect people to the opportunities within their existing organizations—not just jobs but also mentors, learning experiences, stretch assignments, and all the other elements that we need to grow our careers and maximize our talent in an organization.

We are at a time when talent optimization and internal mobility are more critical than ever for business agility and even business continuity. Companies that have full visibility to all the different types of talent at their disposal, with a true line of sight to how work is getting

---

52   Fuel50, "Best Practice Guide to Internal Talent Mobility Playbook," accessed November 8, 2021, https://www.fuel50.com/resources/ best-practice-guide-to-internal-talent-mobility/.

done, by whom, with what skills, performed where and at what value, will have an immediate and significant competitive advantage.

What we think is the future of talent enablement and talent optimization—and what the Fuel50 platform achieves—is employees who are entirely enabled to drive the utilization of their talents. Put that into the talent marketplace, and it will drive talent optimization across the organization so that you do have the right skill and capability where you need it when you need it and in an agile way.

Trane Technologies, a global industrial manufacturing organization, had an internal recruitment rate of 38.7% when they introduced the Fuel50 platform. Just two years later, internal recruitment rates across the business had risen substantially to 55%. This was an incredible achievement for Trane Technologies and their people—not to mention a huge saving on time-consuming and costly external hires.

How To Improve Internal Mobility in Your Organization

| **Reward and recognize leaders** for supporting internal mobility statistics or for attracting internal talent into their team. | **Offer employees opportunities to develop** their skills with gigs and stretch assignments in the absence of open positions. | **Run focus groups with employees** to understand how internal mobility processes could be made easier & improved. | **Implement a best-in-class talent marketplace** solution to connect people with internal opportunities across the business. |

Source: Fuel50, Global Talent Mobility Best Practice Research

STAY AHEAD OF THE GAME TO RETAIN YOUR TALENT

Best-in-class organizations that champion internal talent mobility are more likely to retain their top talent. In our 2020 Fuel50 client data, we found that across our entire client base, employee attrition drops from an average of 24% to 15% churn where a talent marketplace is deployed. But despite being high on the agenda of top strategic HR priorities for organizations everywhere, there is significant room for improvement to internal recruitment practices and internal talent mobility.

As we face shifting talent supply dynamics, there is an urgent imperative for organizations to improve their rates of internal mobility and ensure that internal recruitment and internal talent mobility metrics are being captured and reported. There is an opportunity right now for those that prioritize this to improve talent retention, boost their employer brand, and stand out against the rest.

Best-in-class organizations that champion internal talent mobility are more likely to retain their top talent.

To win the war on talent and significantly improve talent retention statistics, organizations should provide their people with a long-term vision of their evolving role, what other opportunities exist within the organization, and which of those opportunities align with their interests and talents.

HR teams and leaders must also work to understand the goals and aspirations of each of their people and help make them happen. The more people feel supported in their individual goals, the more they will be engaged and feel the organization is doing everything possible to offer them growth experiences, help build their career, and, ultimately, keep them on board.

CUSTOMER JOURNEYS THROUGH CHANGE

Case Study D

Organization: A global audio streaming and media services provider employing 8,000 people worldwide and serving over 400 million people worldwide.

GOAL

To clarify and build a more transparent approach to growing careers by amplifying value exchanges between our talent (skills and aspirations) and growth opportunities (next role, projects, etc.).

BACKGROUND

Client D lacks clarity on how its employees can grow their "careers." Our most recent employee voice results showed career pathing at 75% satisfaction and over 200 comments covering topics from inconsistent manager career development support to too much ambiguity in navigating next steps. All employees and their managers need more guidance to navigate growth with us, particularly where career paths are undefined and global mobility is a challenge. Simultaneously, we are in constant need of talent for new or existing opportunities both long (roles) and short term (bets). We are looking for a solution to clarify and provide more direction while managing expectations about performance and what it takes to progress by leveraging skills as the currency to match growth opportunities with the skills, knowledge, experience, and aspirations of our talent.

WHAT WE SEEK

For every employee to own their careers more effectively by creating clear and tangible paths for growth that they can impact. Every employee will be presented with a personal heat map that connects their skills profile to different types of growth opportunities ranging from rotations to their next possible role. Greater customization of personal profiles, which are already prepopulated with the skills we know they have, will lead to stronger connections in heat maps. Alternatively, leaders or "creators" of growth opportunities from succession planning critical roles (today/tomorrow) to circle teams will be presented with a heat map of internal talent to facilitate value exchanges for the present and future. This will ultimately allow Client D to better plan for and grow talent in the areas needed most in the right time and place.

PILOT STRATEGY

Borrowing the analogy from our own business experience as a two-sided marketplace between consumers and creators, our proposal is to build a two-sided marketplace between employees and growth opportunities to better navigate the next steps in their careers. The connections are made through this skills platform, an employee-driven platform that captures skills (competencies, behaviors, experience, and knowledge) we have today and desire for the future. The growth marketplace ties opportunities to these skills. In addition, our succession planning, critical roles, and open positions are woven together into a fabric with skills as the driving currency for navigating career growth and the next steps. This creates the potential to incorporate artificial intelligence into filing and predicting our talent gaps and employees to have clear guidance to both traditional and less traditional career paths. We believe these journeys will also shift the focus and mentality from job titling and hierarchy to a genuine growth mindset.

The primary objective of a growth marketplace is to facilitate growth exchanges between the skills platform and in growth channels like a career marketplace, succession planning, and tech learning, to name a few. The growth exchanges will build on existing skills in addition to growing into new ones. Each employee will get a personalized heat map of possible next steps; the more they invest and grow their skills profile, the more meaningful the heat map becomes. In addition, creators of growth opportunities will be encouraged to nudge proactively to employees where there's a match between the skills needed for their project and the desires of the employees. Employees will be encouraged to explore the skills we need at Client D with transparency and visibility whenever possible, connecting our strategy to succession planning.

Succession planning currently identifies four boxes that we will expand with underlying top skills needed for critical roles and people today and tomorrow. This exercise combined with others like workforce planning translates into a dynamic view of our current and future skills-haves and gaps. A potential success scenario would leverage these insights to staff a mountain bet/circle based on the skills we need and the skills of employees. Such a transparent and objective approach is meant to inspire confidence and a win-win approach to career planning for both leaders and our talent.

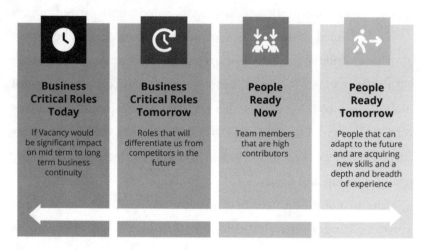

Business Critical Roles Today	Business Critical Roles Tomorrow	People Ready Now	People Ready Tomorrow
If Vacancy would be significant impact on mid term to long term business continuity	Roles that will differentiate us from competitors in the future	Team members that are high contributors	People that can adapt to the future and are acquiring new skills and a depth and breadth of experience

REQUIREMENTS

- Employee skills profile is prepopulated based on current role when a user logs in to the platform for the first time.

- Employee can customize their skills profile (add/remove skills, adjust proficiency level).

- Employee profile includes personalized skills heat map (gap analysis based on current role/skills and aspirations).

- Have the ability for user to provide/receive feedback on skills from peers/manager (360 endorsement).

- Deliver a comprehensive catalogue of skills and skills definitions that can be customized to our language.

- Skills to automatically evolve over time (as employee takes on/completes gig/role, gains proficiency through learning activities, etc.).

- Provide skills-based learning recommendations.

- Match employee to gigs/projects based on skills and aspirations.

- Help user identify and define career path/future opportunities based on their skills and aspirations.

- Opportunity match engine (e.g., AI) to give employee better opportunity matches over time (takes multiple data points into consideration).

- Employees can use search function to find opportunities based on certain criteria and easily get an overview of profile requirements and how their own profile relates to this role/opportunity.

- Provide system that allows mentorship capabilities.

- Provide managers the overview of team's skills profiles and heat map.

- Provide managers the overview of gigs/projects/mentorship/roles or other activity that team members are currently assigned to.

- Provide manager the overview of opportunities that team members have applied for.

- Option to have manager approval as mandatory.

CHAPTER 4

What We Can Learn from the Experts: The Five Rs Driving the Talent Revolution

Liberty looked across her community and saw an urgent need for her people to share their skills, talents, and knowledge. Knowledge could no longer be restricted to a select few. She knew that every single member of her community would benefit from adding to their skill sets— and that in turn would benefit the community as a whole.

She could see a clear need for change in her community, and it had to start from within.

She asked a few more questions of her fellow villagers: Who would you follow or listen to when it comes to people issues? Who would you follow for community-wide decisions?

What she found surprised her: the person the most villagers would listen to on people issues was not the chief of the village or any of the villagers on the council. It was the mother of ten who led the women to the river twice a week to wash clothes and fish. She always had a softly told story to share for every occasion, a story that made everyone listen to her words of wisdom.

Liberty could see this was the leader her community needed. She could see there was a natural leader among them, someone deeply respected by the whole village. Could she be brave enough to float this nontraditional idea to her fellow villagers? Would she actually be able to achieve any change?

The need for a talent revolution is widely acknowledged. Many writers and thinkers across many esteemed institutions and publications have enumerated the factors driving this revolution, which break down into five categories:

- Reengineering

- Reskilling

- Robotics

- Reconstruction

- Reformation

Reengineering: It Takes Resilience

It doesn't take a rocket scientist to know that the coronavirus outbreak and subsequent global lockdown are driving a gigantic change in how we all work. John Kamensky, a fellow at the National Academy of Public Administration, described it like this in a recent issue of *Washington Technology*:

> The response across the economy and in government to COVID-19 has massively accelerated the future of work. The lofty talk about … digital transformation, a remote workforce, distributed teams, telework, is suddenly a reality in both the public and private sectors. Long-standing resistance and silos have been knocked down by a crisis that threatens the very continuity of organizations.[53]

The *Harvard Business Review* also issued a critical call to action for what needs to come next:

> There have been many calls for restructuring how work is done, including making more room for our families and questioning the real value of the eight-hour (or more) work day. Now is a time for companies to step back and re-examine which traditional ways of working exist because of convention, not necessity.[54]

---

53   John M. Kamensky, "The Future of Work Is Here: How 'Distance Work' Is Transforming the Workplace," *Washington Technology*, April 23, 2020, https://washingtontechnology.com/articles/2020/04/23/insights-kamensky-part-1-future-of-work.aspx.

54   Bobbi Thomason and Heather Williams, "What Will Work-Life Balance Look Like after the Pandemic?" *Harvard Business Review*, April 16, 2020, https://hbr.org/2020/04/what-will-work-life-balance-look-after-the-pandemic.

A MASSIVE REENGINEERING OF WORK IS GROWING

Reexamining the traditional ways of working is always a hot topic, but it's even more urgent when the world of work as we know it gets turned upside down due to a global pandemic that impacts everyone, everywhere. One of the big changes to come out of the coronavirus lockdown is likely to be a rebuilding project—really a massive reengineering—of how we will all work in the months and years to come.

It's easy to pin the notion of massive organizational reengineering on the current coronavirus pandemic and lockdown, but in reality, the trend to rebuild the workplace has been accelerating for the last few years as a response to market changes and to allow for more growth. In fact, a 2018 survey of 2,400 employers by London consulting firm Quartz Associates and the *Harvard Business Review* found that 80% of those employers thought that business reengineering would continue at an equal or faster pace for the next five years—and that was well before the global business lockdown kicked in.[55]

But changing the workplace in 2020 won't be anything like it has been in the past 20 years. The business reengineering wave that's developing will be driven, for better or worse, by the many lessons learned by organizations as they have struggled to navigate this global crisis.

Back in March, *Forbes* tried to quantify what some of the issues might be when it comes to reengineering the workplace. Heather McGowan, a future-of-work work strategist and author of *The Adaptation Advantage,* saw it like this:

> If the future of work requires restructured workplaces, redefined roles, rapid learning, and reserves of trust—and

---

55 Stephen Heidari-Robinson, Suzanne Heywood, and Jacquelyn Pless, "How to Make Your Post-Merger Reorg a Success," *Harvard Business Review*, June 13, 2018, https://hbr.org/2018/06/how-to-make-your-post-merger-reorg-a-success.

it does—organizations are being challenged to do all that and more as they address the coronavirus pandemic. While we have long spoken about VUCA (volatile, uncertain, complex, and ambiguous) environments, we are finally and undoubtedly facing one.... Coronavirus, it turns out, might be the great catalyst for business transformation.... [W]here we once saw the future of work unfolding over years, we now believe that with coronavirus as an accelerant, everything we've predicted about the future of work will unfold in months.[56]

CULTURE—THE BACKBONE OF RESILIENT COMPANIES

McGowan believes we are seeing things unfold "that will become a new normal." These changes are all taking place against a backdrop of a fundamental business re-structuring—shifts that are a crisis-driven reengineering of how managers and their workforce operate.

One of the most critical changes she believes is developing comes down to this: **culture is the backbone of resilient companies.**

McGowan writes,

The very survival of a company in the age of the coronavirus is dependent upon a culture that can withstand seismic disruption. A company's culture can be understood in the answers to three fundamental questions:

1. Why do you exist? (*Mission*)

---

56   Heather E. McGowan, "How the Coronavirus Pandemic Is Accelerating the Future of Work," *Forbes*, March 23, 2020, https://www.forbes.com/sites/heathermc-gowan/2020/03/23/the-coronavirus-pandemic-accelerates-the-future-of-work-and-provides-opportunity/.

2. How does the world look differently because you exist? (*Vision*)

3. What will and won't you do to achieve your mission and fulfill your vision? (*Values*)[57]

This is critical in reengineering the workplace. It forces organizations to dig deeply into what they have been saying about their culture and reexamine it in a very basic and fundamental way—a way that they may have never thought about before.

In fact, it challenges companies to step back and examine the philosophy and strategy the organization is built upon and whether it will drive positive change moving ahead.

McGowan describes it this way:

As the pandemic spreads, companies are doubling down on cultures that embrace their commitment to humanity, often at the expense of typical measures of production. In fact, in their nimble responses, they are expanding their capacity....

(Companies that do this) reveal a purpose that lives far beyond the bottom line.... The demands of the coronavirus pandemic were not answered in the production mentality of these companies, but in the nimble capacity to respond in inventive ways, from hiring workers from adjacent industries, training classroom faculty to teach online, equipping employees to work remotely or leveraging expertise to shift production from one product line to another in order to provide the supplies so desperately needed.

This demonstrates a new leadership imperative to focus on inspiring human potential rather than simply driving pro-

---

57 *Ibid.*

ductivity. It is a shift from focusing on what you do **to why and how you do it.**[58]

If all that McGowan writes about—reengineering the workplace with a strong focus on culture and inspiring human potential—sounds familiar, well, that's because it is.

A FAMILIAR CHALLENGE TO REENGINEER THE WORKPLACE

Back in 2015, *Inside HR* published an article about reengineering the workplace for performance. It focused on a Bersin by Deloitte report, and it made this prediction: "Employers will be challenged to re-engineer the workplace, rethink jobs and reshape the way to attract, engage and manage people if they are to drive business performance amidst a growing global economy."[59]

Some of the predictions in the Deloitte report resonate as much today, in the wake of the global shutdown and fledgling business restart, as they did when they were first made five years ago. Here are a few that seem particularly relevant as we reengineer the workplace today:

- **Skills are now currency**; corporate learning takes on increasing importance.

- **Talent analytics and workforce planning become imperative** for competitive advantage.

58   *Ibid.*

59   Donaldson, Craig, "How to Re-Engineer the Workplace for Performance," *Inside HR*, January 6, 2015, https://www.insidehr.com.au/how-to-re-engineer-the-workplace-for-performance/.

- **It's a good time to revisit your HR technology plan ... and look for innovative new solutions** that drive high levels of value.

- **Invest, refocus, and redesign talent acquisition**—leveraging network recruiting, brand reach, and new technologies.[60]

That all sounds good, but a more contemporary Deloitte report from April 2020—The Essence of Resilient Leadership: Business Recovery from COVID-19—also argues that the huge business reengineering that needs to take place must be built on something very basic: a foundation of trust.[61]

TRUST IS THE ESSENTIAL ELEMENT

The new Deloitte report closes with this sobering observation about the workplace reengineering challenge that leaders everywhere are currently facing and how it comes down to one critical element—resilient leadership:

> Sociologists have observed that history does not move linearly, but rather in cycles punctuated by a crisis approximately every 80 years.... Researchers have identified seven such cycles in Anglo-American history since the mid-15th century, with the last crisis being World War II ... 80 years ago.
>
> Each time, the change came with scant warning.... Then sudden sparks ... transformed the public mood, swiftly

---

60 Ibid.

61 Punit Renjen, "The Essence of Resilient Leadership: Business Recovery from COVID-19," Deloitte Insights, April 22, 2020, https://www2.deloitte.com/us/en/ insights/economy/covid-19/guide-to-organizational-recovery-for-senior-executives-heart-of-resilient-leadership.html.

and permanently. Over the next two decades or so, society convulsed. Emergencies required massive sacrifices from a citizenry that responded by putting community ahead of self. *Leaders led, and people trusted them.* As a new social contract was created, people overcame challenges once thought insurmountable—and used the crisis to elevate themselves and their nation to a higher plane of civilization.... [It] is history's great discontinuity. It ends one epoch and begins another.

As resilient leaders embarking on recovery, we embrace trust as the essence of resilient leadership. Invest it wisely and it will yield extraordinary returns.[62]

Reskilling: Now a Global Workforce Imperative

As we enter a new world of work, "reskilling" has gone from being a trending workplace topic to a full-fledged organizational challenge for companies everywhere.

The year 2020 saw a massive shift in the labor market and employment dynamics. The year started off with a talent shortage, and employers were concerned about retention and engagement. By 2021, however, unemployment rates had exploded. This resulted in an abundance of available talent, and organizations have become more concerned about talent optimization to ensure they have the best possible talent in the right roles.

The "Reskilling Revolution," as the World Economic Forum (WEF) calls it, aims "to prepare the global workforce with the skills

---

62   Ibid.

needed to future-proof their careers against the expected displacement of millions of jobs and skills instability as a result of technological change" and "to provide businesses and economies with the skilled labour needed to fulfil the millions of new roles that will be created by the Fourth Industrial Revolution, shifts in the global economy and industrial transitions towards sustainability."[63]

Although reskilling—defined as "the process of learning new skills so you can do a different job, or of training people to do a different job" by the Cambridge English Dictionary—sounds simple enough, companies and organizations around the world are struggling to deal with the issue.[64]

Fuel50's Career Agility & Engagement research found that a whopping 81% of employees feel their skills aren't being fully utilized at work by their organization, and they say they're highly motivated to contribute beyond their current role.[65] Similarly, *Mercer's Global Talent Trends Report* recently highlighted, "Executives believe that 45% of the workforce can adapt to the new world of work, while 78% of employees say they are ready to reskill."[66]

According to the *Harvard Business Review*, the current breakdown is uneven at a time when the need for such investment is greatest:

Employees have demonstrated their willingness and interest; online courses have reported a massive surge of demand

63 World Economic Forum, "The Reskilling Revolution: Better Skills, Better Jobs, Better Education for a Billion People by 2030," January 22, 2020, https://www.weforum.org/press/2020/01/the-reskilling-revolution-better-skills-better-jobs-better-education-for-a-billion-people-by-2030/.

64 "Reskilling," In *Cambridge Dictionary*, accessed June 1, 2021, https://dictionary.cambridge.org/us/dictionary/english/reskilling.

65 "Career Agility & Engagement," Fuel50, April 2019, https://www.fuel50.com/research/career-agility/.

66 *Mercer Global Talent Trends Report*, Mercer, 2020, https://www.fuel50.com/video/mercer-global-talent-trends-report/.

since the pandemic. On the employer side, while some companies are leading the way, Deloitte reports that only 17% of companies have made "meaningful investments" in reskilling initiatives. Particularly as we respond to the long-term effects of the pandemic, more must be done to coordinate and increase these investments.[67]

As the *Wall Street Journal* described it, American companies are struggling to retrain and reskill their workers for the 21st-century workplace. In a 2019 story titled "Why Companies Are Failing at Reskilling," it noted that

> Thousands of companies across [America] are in the thick of a digital revolution that requires them to transform their operations.... But instead of teaching new skills to their current workers, employers often choose the disruption and high costs of layoffs or buyouts.

> Why? Sometimes the required skills aren't easily taught to existing employees, experts say. It's also often because companies have only a hazy sense of what their internal talent is capable of, and migrating large numbers of employees into new positions requires time, money, and commitment.[68]

---

67   Anand Chopra-McGowan and Srinivas B. Reddy, "What Would It Take to Reskill Entire Industries?" *Harvard Business Review*, July 10, 2020, https://hbr.org/2020/07/what-would-it-take-to-reskill-entire-industries.

68   Lauren Weber, "Why Companies Are Failing at Reskilling," *Wall Street Journal*, April 19, 2019, sec. Business, https://www.wsj.com/articles/the-answer-to-your-companys-hiring-problem-might-be-right-under-your-nose-11555689542.

THE LOOMING CHALLENGE

Continuous growth and training are vital to workforce agility and workforce development. And since we're at a time right now where we all need to be agile not only to survive but to thrive, the challenge for organizations is clear, as detailed by the *Harvard Business Review:*

> **Continuous growth and training are vital to workforce agility and workforce development.**

> Companies need to build the next new professional corporate function: reskilling. This capability needs to be elevated and institutionalized like finance, marketing, and risk before it. Many organizations need to add full-fledged systems for continuous learning through teaching, training, and assessing—and they need to do it more effectively and on a larger scale than they have ever attempted before.[69]

If it sounds like a huge undertaking, it is, especially since so many organizations have cut back on corporate training budgets during the pandemic. But increasing spending to reskill your staff is still a better option than the costly alternative—having to recruit and hire new employees with the skill set your organization needs and desires.

That leaves employers with a critically urgent task: investing in reskilling their current workforce. But for many companies, they aren't sure where to start and what to do.

---

69   André Dua, Liz Hilton Segel, and Susan Lund, "It's Time for a C-Level Role Dedicated to Reskilling Workers," *Harvard Business Review*, September 3, 2019, https://hbr.org/2019/09/its-time-for-a-c-level-role-dedicated-to-reskilling-workers.

HOW TO TRANSFORM TO BECOME A SKILLS-BASED ORGANIZATION

We are at a time when talent optimization and internal mobility are more critical than ever for business agility and business continuity. We anticipate interest will continue to grow for skills-based organizations, so to support HR professionals on this journey, we have outlined some critical considerations:

1. Implement a More Flexible, Agile Job Architecture

Many organizations are transitioning to a new operating model of work, moving away from what were hierarchical job architectures to something more agile and fluid. In our recent research, we saw that 35% of organizations surveyed had already simplified to a flat organizational structure, while 25.5% had no intention of doing this at all. A further 24.5% of organizations said they would opt for a more agile-skills and a project-based workforce in the next 12 months.

Flexible, agile organizations are quick to mobilize, nimble, highly collaborative, and responsive; have free-flowing information; and empower people to act. In contrast, traditional job architectures can struggle to stay up to date and respond to the changing needs of the organization. Today's AI-enabled architectures, as supported by Fuel50's Talent Blueprint methodology and market data feeds, provide a mechanism to stay agile and relevant as organizations evolve.

In the first instance, moving to more project-based work units is a start, where skills are matched at the project level, as enabled by the Fuel50 Gigs functionality. This feature creates a valuable starting point, using talent marketplace technology to deliver visibility, keep track of skills, and facilitate more agile working practices by enabling skills matching at the project level. It also lays the foundation for structural changes in the future.

In the future, we are likely to see skills as a foundational unit of currency in the organization. Larry McAlister, VP of global talent at NetApp, is already adopting this future-focused approach. "We really want to say, in our internal marketplace, that skills are the new currency," he says. "There is growth to be had in so many different directions."

2. Take a Skills-Based Approach to Talent Development

Creating a dynamic talent development strategy will enable your organization to understand the skills they need now and in the future, which provides skill transparency to your employees. A skills-based approach enhances talent development strategies by[70]

- Creating visibility of skills across the organization;

- Highlighting skills gaps, allowing organizations to plan upskilling initiatives;

- Creating a common organization-wide approach to skills and talent management; and

- Transforming talent management strategies to include skills management strategies that enable upskilling and reskilling.[71]

3. Implement Agile Methodologies

Agile methodologies are a huge enabler for the success of skills-based organizations. High-performing organizations have adopted agile core values. These prioritize individuals and interactions over processes and

70   Marion Devine, "Navigating to a Skills-Based Approach to Talent Development," the Conference Board, March 19, 2021, https://www.conference-board.org/topics/next-generation-HR/skills-based-to-talent-development.

71   Volker Jacobs, "A Skill-Based Organization of Work: Opportunities & Framework," *AIHR* (blog), October 3, 2018, https://www.aihr.com/blog/a-skill-based-organization-of-work-opportunities-framework/.

tools, prioritize customer collaboration over contract negotiation, and prioritize responding to change over following a plan.[72] A skills-based organization optimizes organizational, talent, and career agility.

Deloitte's Human Capital blog emphasizes that organizations need to consider the following critical principles for a skills-based approach to be successful:[73]

- Create a common language of skills across the organization.

- Performance management needs to include skills application and development.

- Leverage talent marketplaces that match skills to jobs, tasks, projects, gigs, and mentoring assignments.

- Learning and development programs should be designed on skills, not jobs.

- Adopt a skills-based approach to recruiting talent.

- Design compensation policies based on skills.

- Include skills into succession planning.

- Leverage technology to help create visibility and keep track of skills development progress.

The Fuel50 research has identified some transformational capabilities to support organizations in shifting to skills-based organizations. In this report, we identify 15 of our trending capabilities associated with a skills-based organization. We have found that these

72 Ravin Jesuthasan and John Boudreau, "Work without Jobs," *MIT Sloan Management Review*, January 5, 2021, https://sloanreview.mit.edu/article/work-without-jobs/.

73 Michael Griffiths, "The Skills-Based Organization: Fueling the 21st Century Enterprise with Skills," Deloitte, September 14, 2021, http://www2.deloitte.com/us/en/blog/human-capital-blog/2021/skills-based-talent-strategies.html.

capabilities need to be embedded into three levels (individual, leadership, and organizational) to successfully transition from a job-based to a skills-based organization.

- **Individual enablers:** mental elasticity, agility, self-development, technological savvy, interdisciplinary knowledge

- **Leadership capabilities:** agile leadership, change leader, empowering others, skills management, distributed agile teams

- **Organizational strategic imperatives:** skills transparency, agile business strategy, VUCA readiness, agile workforce, disruptive innovation

THREE SOLUTIONS TO CONSIDER

Other experts have also outlined a number of ways to approach the problem. Randstad recently made the case for organizations investing in what they call "internal redeployment solutions." There are three components to this approach:

1. **A sharp focus on "intelligent" redeployment.** *From Randstad:* "An increased use of ... analytics and data are now allowing companies to address talent shortage and look at redeployment in a new, more 'intelligent' way, making redeployment more effective than ever before.... While redeploying employees has been a strategy used by companies over the last several years, the use of HR analytics offers businesses a wealth of information about their human capital. Talent analytics offers recruiters and leadership teams deeper insight into a company's talent portfolio, allowing for more informed hiring decisions to be made."

2. **A shift from an external focus (recruiting and hiring) to an internal focus (training and reskilling)**. *From Randstad*: "According to Gartner Inc., companies will need to shift from external hiring to training their current workforces to address the increasing global skills shortage. A 2018 survey conducted of 137 senior executives showed growing concerns of talent shortage compared to recent years, with 63 percent of respondents indicating that a skills shortage was one of their top concerns for 2019."

3. **Systematically engaging in more "internal mobility" of employees**. *From Randstad*: "Since the global skills shortage is expecting to grow in coming years, an alternative to layoffs and loss of talent is internal redeployment. Redeployment keeps your already-trained and skilled employees available for new roles that may open up within an organization, resulting in a quicker fill-time."[74]

McKinsey also recently made the case for investing in building workforce skills now. They highlight the following six steps to reskilling:

1. **Rapidly identify the skills your recovery business model depends on.** *From McKinsey:* "Specify the quantity and type of people you need. For example, if you are moving from in-store sales to predominately home deliveries, your tech team and logistics coordinators will have a greater impact on the new strategy than they did on the old one. They may also

---

74 Randstad, "Redeployment on the Rise as Skills Shortage Persists," June 8, 2020, https://www.randstad.com/workforce-insights/talent-management/redeployment-rise-skills-shortage-persists/.

need a different skill set to facilitate the increase in demand and customer expectations."

2. **Build employee skills critical to your new business model.** *From McKinsey:* "Start upskilling the critical workforce pools that will drive a disproportionate amount of value in your adjusted business model. The first step is to build a no-regrets skill set—a tool kit that will be useful no matter how an employee's specific role may evolve."

3. **Launch tailored learning journeys to close critical skill gaps.** *From McKinsey:* "As companies prepare to reimagine and ramp up their business models, it is important to go deeper on strategic workforce planning. Leaders need a detailed view not only of the core activities that critical groups will begin undertaking in the next 12 to 18 months but also of which skills each of these groups will need."

4. **Start now, test rapidly, and iterate.** *From McKinsey:* "Organizations shouldn't launch reskilling initiatives and then disband them after the crisis passes; whatever talent reskilling or redeployment you do now should also be used to expand your reskilling capabilities going forward."

5. **Act like a small company to have a big impact.** *From McKinsey:* "Smaller companies tend to have a clearer view of their skill deficiencies, so they're better at prioritizing the gaps they need to address and at selecting the right candidates for reskilling. That's not to say larger organizations can't be agile when it comes to reskilling, just that it can be harder for them."

6. **Protect learning budgets (or regret it later).** *From McKinsey:* "Companies should not cut their employee-training budgets. According to the Training Industry Report, US data during and after the Great Recession showed a significant drop in overall training expenditures in 2009 and 2010, followed by a surge in 2011 and a drop back to 2008 levels in 2012. What this tells us is that if companies cut their learning budgets now, they're only delaying their investment, not netting a saving—especially since the current crisis will require a larger skill shift than the 2008 financial crisis did."[75]

When reskilling becomes a priority, there is more opportunity for internal talent mobility and workforce agility within an organization. When employees have more internal mobility, ongoing training and reskilling, and clear career paths so they can see where their career is going, it drives overall morale, and retention grows as a result. In addition, it helps build your employer brand and sends a strong message that you really *do* put your employees first.

> **When reskilling becomes a priority, there is more opportunity for internal talent mobility and workforce agility within an organization.**

---

75 Sapana Agrawal, Aaron De Smet, Sébastien Lacroix, and Angelika Reich, "To Emerge Stronger from the COVID-19 Crisis, Companies Should Start Reskilling Their Workforces Now," McKinsey & Company, May 7, 2020, https://www.mckinsey.com/business-functions/organization/our-insights/to-emerge-stronger-from-the-covid-19-crisis-companies-should-start-reskilling-their-workforces-now.

Robots Won't Replace Us—As Long As We Can Leverage AI's "Productivity Potential"

This might be hard to remember today, but back in January 2020, the biggest workplace concern was *not* coping with COVID-19. No, in those carefree days before face masks, lockdowns, and social distancing, the biggest challenge facing the future workplace was something that almost seems quaint today.

Back then, the biggest worry was something very different—how were we going to cope with the rise of artificial intelligence (AI) in the workplace, and what did it mean for our jobs?

Looking back at 2019 and early 2020, there seemed to be a frightening story about AI every other day. For example, an Oxford Economics report estimated that artificial intelligence would displace 20 million manufacturing jobs worldwide.[76] Another story in *Business Insider* quotes a Cornell University professor who told the US Congress that upward of 1.3 million bank workers could lose their jobs because of AI.[77] Probably the most frightening prediction of all came from a Brookings Institution study that estimated that a

---

76 "How Robots Change the World: What Automation Really Means for Jobs and Productivity," Oxford Economics, June 2019, https://www.oxfordeconomics.com/resource/how-robots-change-the-world.

77 Allana Akhtar, "The 2020s Could Be an Apocalyptic Decade for Wall Street as Artificial Intelligence Takes over the Most Popular Jobs in Finance," *Business Insider*, December 9, 2019, https://www.businessinsider.com/banking-jobs-remain-popular-despite-the-threat-of-automation-2019-4.

whopping 88 million jobs could be impacted by automation (AI) in the next 10 years.[78]

UNLOCKING THE "PRODUCTIVITY POTENTIAL" OF AI

Yes, life may be very different today than it was on New Year's Day 2020, but this much is true: even as vaccines are administered and coronavirus concerns fade away, the impact of artificial intelligence on the workplace will still be with us for many years into the future.

The *Harvard Business Review* spelled this out in a March 2020 article titled "AI Is Changing Work—and Leaders Need to Adapt." In it, IBM's chief economist Martin Fleming wrote,

> As AI is increasingly incorporated into our workplaces and daily lives, it is poised to fundamentally upend the way we live and work. Concern over this looming shift is widespread. A recent survey of 5,700 Harvard Business School alumni found that 52% of even this elite group believe the typical company will employ fewer workers three years from now.
>
> The advent of AI poses new and unique challenges for business leaders. They must continue to deliver financial performance while simultaneously making significant investments in hiring, workforce training, and new technologies that support productivity and growth. These seemingly

---

78 Mark Muro, Robert Maxim, and Jacob Whiton, "Automation and Artificial Intelligence: How Machines Are Affecting People and Places," *Brookings* (blog), January 24, 2019, https://www.brookings.edu/research/automation-and-artificial-intelligence-how-machines-affect-people-and-places/.

competing business objectives can make for difficult, often agonizing, leadership decisions.[79]

Fleming believes that there are three key strategies business leaders need to focus on if they are to unlock "the productivity potential" that artificial intelligence can bring to their organizations. They are

1. **Rebalancing resources**. *Fleming's view*: "Our research shows that only 2.5% of jobs include a high proportion of tasks suitable for machine learning.... Most tasks will still be best performed by humans ... and new tasks will emerge that require workers to exercise new skills.... As this shift occurs, business leaders will need to reallocate capital accordingly ... (because) training and re-skilling employees will very likely require temporarily removing workers from revenue-generating activities."

2. **Investing in workforce reskilling.** *Fleming's view:* "Millions of workers will need to be retrained or reskilled as a result of AI over the next three years, according to a recent IBM Institute for Business Value study.... As tasks requiring intellectual skill, insight and other uniquely human attributes rise in value, executives ... will also need to focus on preparing workers for the future by fostering and growing 'people skills' such as judgment, creativity and the ability to communicate effectively."

3. **Advancing new models of education and lifelong learning on a larger scale**. *Fleming's view*: "Our research shows that technology can disproportionately impact the demand and

---

79   Martin Fleming, "AI Is Changing Work—and Leaders Need to Adapt," *Harvard Business Review*, March 24, 2020, https://hbr.org/2020/03/ai-is-changing-work-and-leaders-need-to-adapt.

earning potential for mid-wage workers, causing a squeeze on the middle class.... New models of education and pathways to continuous learning can help address the growing skills gap, providing members of the middle class, as well as students and a broad array of mid-career professionals, with opportunities to build in-demand skills. Investment in ALL forms of education is key."

YES, AI WILL HELP US DO OUR JOBS BETTER

If there is a silver lining to the global pandemic, it may be this: regardless of all the fears about what artificial intelligence might do to human jobs, the coronavirus lockdown has shown that robots and technology aren't going to displace millions of workers anytime soon.

"While fears of being replaced by a machine are understandable based on history ... AI is being introduced into the workplace to augment and help existing employees do their jobs better, not replace them," according to a *TechRepublic* story titled "How AI is Impacting the Workplace."[80]

That may sound good, but it may also leave you confused at how AI has suddenly morphed into something that *won't* chew through millions of jobs as so many have predicted. Is that really possible? As *TechRepublic* explains, "The reason for this may be very straightforward: as impressive as it is (think self-driving cars or Google's DeepMind beating human Go champions) technology just isn't capable of doing what humans can do. At least not yet."

---

80   Allen Bernard, "How AI Is Impacting the Workplace," *TechRepublic*, February 18, 2020, https://www.techrepublic.com/article/how-ai-is-impacting-the-workplace/.

And *Wired* magazine is even more blunt when they ask, in the wake of so many workplaces shut down due to the coronavirus, "Why haven't the machines saved us yet?"

Here's the point they make when it comes to the growth of AI and its impact on people and their jobs:

> This economic catastrophe is blowing up the myth of the worker robot and AI takeover. We've been led to believe that a new wave of automation is here, made possible by smarter AI and more sophisticated robots.… Yet our economy still craters without human workers, because the machines are far, far away from matching our intelligence and dexterity.
>
> You're more likely to have a machine automate *part* of your job, not destroy your job entirely. Moving from typewriters to word processors made workers more efficient. Increasingly sophisticated and sensitive robotic arms can now work side-by-side on assembly lines with people without flinging our puny bodies across the room, doing the heavy lifting and leaving the fine manipulation of parts to us.
>
> The machines have their strengths—literally in this case— and the humans have theirs.[81]

EMPLOYEES STILL BRING A *LOT* OF VALUE

If you think about it, robots and artificial intelligence shouldn't be any more frightening than the transition from flip phones to smart phones, where we suddenly found that not only could we still call and

---

text but also had an incredibly powerful device that was more like a hand-held computer.

It did a lot of the same things a flip phone did, but it made us a lot more efficient and productive as well.

TechRepublic believes this too, but they also add this caveat from Beena Ammanath, AI managing director at Deloitte Consulting. She says,

> For now at least, AI is not displacing employees. And won't any time soon. In some cases, however, companies are re-training their employees to train the AI the organization is deploying so it understands things like emotional intelligence. This is a good example of what is actually more likely to happen, and has happened in the past, as new technology is introduced into the workforce: jobs will change.
>
> There are some jobs that will be displaced, that just won't be relevant … (but) there's definitely a lot of organizations that, more than displacing the workforce, will think of "*How do we re-skill them so that they can continue to tap into the domain, the core knowledge that exists within those employees?*" There's a lot of value in the domain knowledge that these employees possess.[82]

Reconstruction: Communication Is Key

The workplace is always changing, but with the advancement of technology in the 21st century, the rate of change seems to have acceler-

---

ated and is moving more rapidly than ever before—especially over the course of and in the wake of the pandemic.

People are creatures of habit, and nowhere is that more evident than on the job, where employees like a familiar routine where they feel comfortable and confident that they know what they're doing—and can keep on doing it that way. That's why a workplace restructuring can be so terribly frightening and stressful.

Now is the era of reconstruction, not restructuring, which was a heavily emotion-laden term last century. Reconstructing is when an employer changes the nature and functions of the organization's structure to deliver on its purpose and strategic goals. This can include horizontal reconstruction—when a worker's current job requirements are modified to include some new tasks performed in other jobs on the same level—or vertical reconstruction—when a position is given responsibilities and tasks previously performed at higher levels.

Restructuring of jobs and responsibilities is usually associated with employee layoffs that happen in a merger or large corporate-driven action in response to business conditions, but numerous studies have found that just about *any* kind of change, especially restructuring of your job or your workplace, is highly stressful.

FIVE THINGS THAT STRESS WORKERS DURING RESTRUCTURING

When workers are stressed, they don't feel confident and comfortable anymore, and that usually means they're not as productive for as long as it takes to adjust and get confident and comfortable again.

The Guardian newspaper listed the five most common reasons that people feel stressed during a period of change at work. See if these sound familiar:

- **Fear of personal failure within a new structure:** "It will never work out for me. I won't be able to do it."

- **Preferring the familiar, old routine:** "The old way was much better, we knew what we were doing before."

- **Denial of the reasons for change:** "Why did we have to do this anyway? I can't see how this will improve anything."

- **Unwillingness to learn new systems and processes:** "I already know everything I need to know to do my job, nothing new can help me."

- **Fear of the unknown:** "I don't know what it will be like for any of us, but I know we will all be worse off."[83]

What scares employees about a restructuring, besides the fear of the unknown, is the worry that sometimes, a workplace restructuring can go horribly wrong, as it did at Nokia, the famous Finnish mobile phone maker that once dominated the global cell phone market.[84]

WHEN RESTRUCTURING GOES TERRIBLY WRONG

As the *South China Morning Post* wrote, "For many years the name Nokia was synonymous with mobile communications. It took only two decades for the Finnish firm to help create and dominate the industry—with a 40% global market share at its height—before

---

83 Mandy Rutter, "Coping with Stress: A Survival Guide to Restructuring and Redundancy at Work," *The Guardian*, July 28, 2014, http://www.theguardian.com/careers/cope-stress-survival-guide-restructuring-redundancy-change-work.

84 Mistina Picciano, "The Demise of Nokia—A Cautionary Tale of Restructuring Gone Wrong | ODI," *OD Innovator Magazine* (blog), June 29, 2018, https://odinnovator.com/restructuring/demise-nokia-cautionary-tale-restructuring-gone-wrong/.

crashing out in a spectacular fashion with the fire sale of its mobile phones business to Microsoft."[85]

What caused Nokia's crash? It came down to two critical issues that impact a lot of organizations:

- **Nokia refused to evolve, they lost their lead, and their downward trend continued for years,** according to the *Helsinki Times.* The company's inward, operational focus "marked a drastic change from the innovative and entrepreneurial approach that had powered the company's success during the early 1990s."[86]

- **A company restructuring in 2004 resulted in a "matrix structure" that only made Nokia's problems worse**. "Key team members left, and collaboration across business units collapsed," according to the *Morning Post.* "Even so, Nokia attempted three additional reorganizations before finally selling its mobile phone business to Microsoft in 2013."[87]

If Nokia is a prime example of restructuring gone wrong, it's important to remember that organizations are changing and evolving all the time. More often than not, restructuring jobs and the larger workplace is a necessary course correction that's simply part of the ongoing evolution that *all* organizations face.

When done right, a company restructuring not only helps a business reconfigure its strategic alignment but also helps to improve

85 Yves Doz and Keeley Wilson, "Why the Mighty Fail—Lessons from Nokia," *South China Morning Post*, February 2, 2018, https://www.scmp.com/business/companies/article/2131615/why-mighty-fail-lessons-nokia.

86 "Whatever Happened to Nokia? The Rise and Decline of a Giant," *Helsinki Times*, October 30, 2019, https://www.helsinkitimes.fi/business/16809-whatever-happened-to-nokia-the-rise-and-decline-of-a-giant.html.

87 Doz and Wilson.

employee satisfaction because it addresses issues that hinder employees from doing their best work.

However, there are potential problems if the restructuring isn't carefully planned and executed. Some of the potential issues are employee insecurity about their new role, worry over their modified duties, and the time needed to adjust and rework job descriptions. In addition, there may be some overlap in positions and uncertainty over responsibilities for certain tasks.

THE KEY TO MAKING *ANY* RESTRUCTURING GO RIGHT

Yes, a workplace restructuring at just about *any* level is difficult and stressful for everyone, but a number of studies have found that there is one simple thing that helps to make *all* of them go better.

Simply put, it's communication.

A 2016 report in *Medical Daily* was very pointed about this. They reported that researchers found companies that provided continuous communication about the restructuring transition, and had proper training for staff who took on new responsibilities, had a positive impact on the well-being of employees.[88]

The report also said that

> Organizations, managers, and employees should be supported in dealing with changes in a healthy way, for example by training, coaching, and other on-the-job programs aimed at individual, group, and management level. Researchers and occupational and human resource ... practitioners should

---

88   Steve Smith, "Employee Satisfaction: Corporate Restructuring Can Negatively Affect Employee Wellbeing, Even If No Jobs Are Lost," *Medical Daily*, February 2, 2016, https://www.medicaldaily.com/corporate-restructuring-well-being-employee-satisfaction-job-cuts-371936.

work together in developing interventions and evaluating the intervention process and its impact on well-being and company results.[89]

At its core, all of this is about communicating early and often during a restructuring. In fact, business leaders told the *Harvard Business Review* that the key to a successful restructuring is to not only communicate often but to "communicate much more than you would think is natural."[90]

Iain Conn, the CEO of Centrica who has led three major reorgs, told *HBR* how important constant communication is: "You need to treat people with respect and dignity, being transparent and telling them what is happening and when. You need to keep communicating with people. The biggest mistake is to communicate once and think you are done. You should keep communicating, even things people have heard already, to reinforce the message and ensure it sinks in."[91]

If you're considering any kind of workplace reconstruction to become more strategic or purpose aligned, or employee role restructuring, you better get communicating now.

When organizations undergo any kind of change or job restructuring, no matter how big or small, everyone is affected—even those who aren't personally involved in the change. Communicating clearly, consistently, and frequently is key to getting through the

---

89   Ibid.

90   Stephen Heidari-Robinson and Suzanne Heywood, "The Two Biggest Communication Blunders During a Reorg," *Harvard Business Review*, October 20, 2016, https://hbr.org/2016/10/the-two-biggest-communication-blunders-during-a-reorg.

91   Ibid.

process and returning everyone to a state where they are once again confident and comfortable in doing the best job possible.

That's the end goal and the outcome you are looking for. If you're considering *any* kind of workplace reconstruction to become more strategic or purpose aligned, or employee role restructuring, you better get communicating *now*.

Reformation: Encouraging a More Powerful Employee Voice

Here's another workplace truism that shouldn't come as a great surprise: employees who feel they can speak up about workplace issues are much more successful at their jobs. If we feel that this may be a good time to rethink and reform the workplace, ensuring that employees have more of a voice in doing so may be a good place to start.

"Employee voice isn't just a warm and cuddly agenda—it's a hard-edged agenda about making sure your company is productive and innovative," says Matthew Taylor, chief executive of the Royal Society for the Encouragement of Arts, Manufactures and Commerce (RSA), in the UK's *HR Magazine*.[92] Taylor believes that listening to employees' voices creates happier workers, a "more collegiate environment between managers and staff," and boosts productivity.

He's absolutely right about that; however, here is another workplace truism that also isn't surprising: only 25%—one out of four—of employees feel that they are able to freely express themselves at work.

---

92 Rachel Sharp, "Breaking the Silence: Employee Voice," *HR Magazine*, July 9, 2018, https://www.hrmagazine.co.uk/articles/breaking-the-silence-employee-voice/.

THE KEY TO BUILDING A STRONG COMPANY CULTURE

This data point comes from a 2019 research study titled *Talking About Voice: Employees' Experiences* from the London-based Chartered Institute of Personnel and Development (CIPD), a professional association for HR management.[93]

This shouldn't be breaking news for any manager or business leader, because the concept of employee "voice" is at the heart of building a strong company culture. As Heather Mueller wrote on the Emplify blog, giving employees more voice in their organization is crucial:

> A growing body of research indicates that a key indicator of organizational success is a company's ability to make employees feel heard.
>
> Giving employees a share of voice is a critical component of establishing a workforce that's happy, productive, and engaged. It's not until an employee is convinced that his suggestions play an integral role in decision making that they become willing to communicate ideas, concerns, and opinions.
>
> Employee voice is what makes it possible to build a corporate culture around respect and shared values.[94]

93   Helen Shipton, Daniel King, Nikolas Pautz, and Louisa Baczor, "Talking about Voice: Employees' Experiences," Chartered Institute of Personnel and Development, February 2019, https://www.cipd.co.uk/Images/talking-about-voice_employees-experiences_tcm18-54482.pdf.

94   Heather Mueller, "Why Is Employee Voice So Important?" Emplify, March 3, 2017, https://emplify.com/blog/why-is-employee-voice-so-important/.

Heather Mueller is on to something here, because "respect and shared values" are critical factors in any important endeavor. They're also two great reasons to appreciate why fostering a stronger and more consistent employee voice is so important—and why we need to make it a key part of any agenda to rework, restructure, and ultimately reform the workplace.

"EMPLOYEE VOICE ISN'T JUST A WARM AND CUDDLY AGENDA"

So what is "employee voice?" Put simply, it is "ensuring that everyone working in an organization is able to talk or write about what they see as important," and it's also a "vital enabler for business performance."[95]

> CIPD adds a few more layers to that description, making the case that employee voice is [T]he means by which employees communicate views on employment and organizational issues to their employer. It's the main way employees can influence matters that affect them at work. For employers, effective voice contributes toward innovation, productivity and business improvement. For employees, it often results in increased job satisfaction, greater influence and better opportunities for development.[96]

However, it's also important to keep in mind that encouraging employees to use their voice isn't just a nice thing to do but is a critically important part of your larger workplace culture.

Forbes says that "culture is the binding force that holds a workplace together, and its foundation is the voice of employee. In this new

---

95   Jon Ingham, "The Benefits of Employee Voice at Work," Workstars, accessed May 31, 2021, https://www.workstars.com/recognition-and-engagement-blog/2015/05/12/the-benefits-of-employee-voice-at-work/.

96   Shipton et al.

way of working, it is more important than ever for organizations and leaders to stay in tune with how their employees are feeling."[97]

But reforming the workplace is a serious business right now, and here's another reason why the voice of employees is a crucial part of it: employees are your early warning device for leaders to know what critical issues need attending to.

"Employee voice is the cheapest smoke alarm you can buy," says David MacLeod, cochair of the UK's Employee Engagement Task Force and coauthor of the MacLeod Report.[98]

"There are only four real ways to improve a business and they all require and benefit from employee voice," he continues. "One is through employees innovating, the second is to open up new markets, the third is to do things more efficiently, and the fourth is customer service."

MacLeod says it is the employees on the ground who hear from customers and get a good sense of their mood. If the voice of those employees is heard by managers, the organization can "catch things early" before they escalate to the point of no return.[99]

MAKE SURE THE VOICES ARE HEARD

Clearly, the debate over how to give employees a stronger voice is not clear cut, and there are a number of different approaches. "What matters is that workers are respected, their voices are heard, and they feel empowered to influence decisions," says Taylor in the UK's *HR*

---

97 Eric Mosley, "Amplifying the Voice of the Employee As Work-places Adjust to the New Normal," *Forbes*, May 22, 2020, https://www.forbes.com/sites/ericmosley/2020/05/22/amplifying-the-voice-of-the-employee-as-workplaces-adjust-to-the-new-normal/.

98 Sharp.

99 Ibid.

Magazine. "The way you do it can vary from firm to firm or industry to industry."[100]

But sometimes, employee voices are stifled, and at other times, they are stolen. "Organizations must be on guard against 'stealing' employees' voices in exchange for a paycheck," writes David Zinger in the Saba blog. "The days of show up, keep your head down and your mouth shut are not tenable" for encouraging good work in 2020 and beyond.[101]

This is truer today than ever, as recent movements like #MeToo and Black Lives Matter have emphasized how often voices—especially the voices of women and nonwhite people—are suppressed by traditional power structures. As we all become more aware of these issues, it is vital for companies to make sure their workplace culture allows employees to speak up—even if those conversations are challenging or uncomfortable.

Zinger also adds this important perspective:

> Our voice is human. Yet we often refer to employee voice as if it is a single entity-employee voice. There are many employee voices—a pluralism of experiences, perspectives, expressions, ideas and evaluations. The pervasive pluralism of voices can add rich understanding to organizations even if that understanding may at first be disruptive to the organization.

Absorb all of that, and perhaps you will be able to reform your own workplace by better encouraging, and leveraging, the voice of your own employees.

---

100 Ibid.

101 David Zinger, "Employee Engagement and Employee Voice: Do You Hear What I Hear?" *Saba* (blog), January 29, 2018, https://www.saba.com/es/blog/employee-engagement-and-employee-voice-do-you-hear-what-i-hear.

With these five Rs driving momentum, it is clear that the time for revolution is now. But what does a revolution look like? What makes it successful? And if it's so imperative, why haven't we had one already?

To answer these questions, we'll look at some of the most successful revolutions throughout history—and see what they can teach us about revolutionizing talent practices.

CUSTOMER JOURNEYS THROUGH CHANGE

Case Study E

Organization: A British multinational banking and financial services company, headquartered in England, with 85,000 employees around the globe.

The talent marketplace should enable the bank to grow a future workforce that is engaged, skilled for the future, ready for a cultural shift to embrace internal mobility and development.

Through the talent marketplace, we are seeking to address several problem statements:

- Improve our people's perceptions of career, growth, and development opportunities

- Accelerate our ability to help our people upskill and reskill to build a future-ready workforce

- Make it easy to locate, connect, and deploy people who have the skills needed in areas of biggest opportunity

- New approaches to developing and deploying talent

- Create an inclusive, transparent, and open approach to showcasing career and development opportunities on offer

- How might we enable people to get insight into how they can manage their own careers and progression in the future world of work

The bank is looking for a solution to develop internal talent mobility by matching employees across opportunities including internal job openings, part-time projects, and mentorships via the use of technology.

The overall outcome for our global bank is

1. to match supply and demand of skills and opportunities in order to create development and engagement opportunities facilitated by technology and

2. to identify potential critical talent across the whole organization and validate, develop, and mobilize potential employees for roles and to inform strengths and development priorities.

C H A P T E R 5

The Psychology of Revolutions

To figure out how to bring about real change, Liberty knew she needed inspiration beyond her village. In the community hall was a dusty library of old, battered books. After she had completed her chores for the day, Liberty read voraciously. She read every philosophy and history book she could find to see what she could learn about successful change strategies. She read everything from Plato and Aristotle to nihilists like Nietzsche to humanists like Jean-Paul Sartre, along with books describing the works of revolutionary leaders like Gandhi, Nelson Mandela, Karl Marx, and Winston Churchill.

She had one burning question in her mind as she read: How did these people create change? How did they influence their societies to make a real, substantial, and lasting difference?

There are countless change principles, methodologies and models used in HR to help guide organizations through transformation—and frankly, I'm bored with them. They've all been around for ages. The most frequently used models—such as Lewin's Change Management Model, the ADKAR Model, Kotter's eight-step change model, the Bridges Transition Model, and the McKinsey 7-S model—all originated in the 1980s and '90s (although they are all evolving and sustaining).

A quick online search shows another interesting thing: there are many articles on change and transformation published through 2019 and then nothing in 2020—almost as though we were so in the thick of dealing with rapid change that there was no time to think strategically about change management.

Well, now is that time—and now is the time to look at change in a fresh way. I believe we can actually find a fresh perspective on change and transformation by looking to history: to the movements and revolutions that have effectively implemented change in our world.

When we look at successful revolutions throughout human history, how did they build the momentum to create change? What made them successful? What can we take forward from those revolutions into our practices in HR? What lessons can we apply from successful revolutionaries to create effective change?

Deep Belief and Unrelenting Commitment

When we look at what we can learn from the world's great revolutionaries, we can see that there are some commonalities across great revolutionaries and great change agents.

The number one facet that unifies the true revolutionaries of recent history is a deep belief and unrelenting commitment to a cause. Think of Mahatma Gandhi's unwavering belief in and unfaltering pursuit of India's independence from colonial rule, achieved through nonviolent resistance. Gandhi was one of the most effective change agents and revolutionary leaders of recent times.

The number one facet that unifies the true revolutionaries of recent history is a deep belief and unrelenting commitment to a cause.

His revolutionary ideals were so powerful he inspired movements for civil rights and freedom across the world—including that of Martin Luther King Jr., whose unrelenting commitment to the Civil Rights Movement, advanced through nonviolence and civil disobedience, was inspired both by his Christian beliefs and the nonviolent activism of Gandhi.

The socialist revolutionary and political critic Karl Marx also epitomizes a strong, relentless vision and a powerful voice. In his hugely influential writings, including *The Communist Manifesto* and *Das Kapital*, Marx espoused a belief system that called for the proletariat to rise up and topple capitalism, bringing about socioeconomic emancipation in a classless society of true equality and opportunity for all.

This classless society Marx envisioned is part of what inspired us to create the talent marketplace: a free, inclusive for all, equitable, fair, and transparent marketplace where everyone in a business can contribute their skills and talents with equal visibility to opportunity—as Marx said, "From each according to his abilities, to each according to his needs."

If we look to more recent business revolutionaries like Elon Musk and Richard Branson, we can also see an unrelenting commitment to better and new ways of doing things. Elon Musk has not been afraid to dream big and aim high and disrupt the status quo along the way. As *Business Today* put it, "[Musk's company] Tesla doesn't play the game—it has completely reinvented it, single handedly forcing every automobile organization to adopt electric vehicle plans for the future. Fully harnessing the magic of fantasies dreamt up by children playing with toy cars and plastic rockets, Elon Musk, Tesla, and SpaceX have completely reinvented the trajectory of the human race."[102]

Musk is also not afraid to take a sometimes-contentious stance on current workplace issues, whether in the form of Twitter comments like, "If you are not contributing in a meeting, then leave," or in taking a stand on the debate around returning to the in-person workplace. He recently moved to end all remote work at Tesla, declaring, "If you don't show up, we will assume you have resigned."[103]

From an early age, Branson wanted to be an entrepreneur, and he built his vision to now span 400 companies in the Virgin Group. Branson was able to accomplish this because of his revolutionary spirit. "I think there sort of almost needs to be a perpetual revolution going on within a company," he says, "because if you don't have that happening, somebody out there is going to do it to you."[104] And he brings this spirit not just to his businesses but to his vision of how companies can improve the world:

102 Akshita Gandra, "From Laughable to Revolutionary: Elon Musk, Tesla, and SpaceX," *Business Today Online Journal*, July 3, 2019, https://journal.businesstoday.org/bt-online/2019/from-laughable-to-revolutionary-elon-musk-tesla-and-spacex.

103 BBC News, "Elon Musk Declares End to Remote Working at Tesla," June 2, 2022, sec. Business, https://www.bbc.com/news/business-61666339.

104 Lydia Belanger, "Richard Branson: There Needs to Be 'Perpetual Revolution' Within Your Business," *Entrepreneur*, January 17, 2017, https://www.entrepreneur.com/article/287865.

"If we can get every single company in the word to adopt a problem and use their entrepreneurial skills to try to overcome a problem—or two—most of the problems in the world will be solved," Branson said, noting that he has seen many humanitarian crises improve throughout his lifetime and is optimistic about the future. "I think there is a danger that if we don't do things like this and we just leave it up to governments and we leave it up to the social sector, that the world won't get fixed."[105]

Musk's and Branson's visions have literally taken them out of this world, as they are both now engaged in a race to space. They are both visionaries, big thinkers, adventurers, game-changing entrepreneurs, and we have much to learn from them.

Rallying the People

When we think of revolutions, of movements that effected great change in the world, we usually think of the great revolutionary leaders—charismatic, visionary men and women like Martin Luther King Jr., Mahatma Gandhi, Dolores Huerta, Cesar Chavez. While these leaders were indeed visionaries, what made their revolutions successful was the fact they were *leaders*: they were able to unite people together into a groundswell of momentum that made change unstoppable.

A successful outcome takes commitment from a lot of people. Even the most charismatic, visionary, engaging leader won't get very far in their revolution without the support of the people, without a movement—or, to use HR speak, without stakeholder engagement.

---

105 Ibid.

The National Farm Workers Association, which became the United Farm Workers, one of the most successful workers' rights movements in the United States, became so successful in part because its cofounders, Cesar Chavez and Dolores Huerta, brought many different stakeholders together. As Matt Garcia, author of *From the Jaws of Victory: The Triumph and Tragedy of Cesar Chavez and the Farm Worker Movement*, writes,

> By using community organizing efforts begun in the wake of World War II, [Chavez] and his early allies forged a broad, new coalition of workers, students, social justice activists, and religious affiliates. Throughout the 1960s and the first half of the 1970s, the United Farm Workers won most of their battles by leveraging this diversity. Farm owners, on the other hand, remained committed to ethnic cliques and business models that made it difficult for them to communicate a common message.[106]

How did revolutionary leaders like Chavez, King, and Gandhi get so many people to follow their vision? By starting, as Simon Sinek says, with *why*.

Too often, organizations don't take time for the *why*. They take it for granted. But it's essential to start with *why*. Revolutionary leaders like Mahatma Gandhi and Martin Luther King Jr. created a vision of a better future through their thoughtful, clever language—an inspiring *why* that people could rally around and relentlessly commit to.

Conceptualizing and clearly articulating the *why* behind change is how you get a groundswell of support across an organization. You need people to buy into the vision of a better way of doing things.

---

106 Matt Garcia, "Successes and Failures of Cesar Chavez and the United Farm Workers Union," Utne Reader, January 17, 2013, https://www.utne.com/politics/cesar-chavez-united-farm-workers-union-ze0z1301zwar/.

You need them not just to follow orders but to actually engage and believe in the change.

According to *Forbes*, "The U.S. wastes $2 trillion on change initiatives each year, because too many leaders try to 'change by decree.' Making people change leads to compliance that doesn't last. To achieve lasting change, there must be emotional buy-in from employees. As human beings, we don't change our behaviors if we don't care about the reason for doing it."[107]

Harvard Business Review reports similar findings: "A review of transformations across industries reveals a common theme: Successful transformations realign the organization to a singular vision; failed endeavors typically do not."[108]

As *Forbes* continues, "The best way to drive a desire for behavior change is for employees to understand the *what* and *why* of the change."[109]

Get *Everybody* On Board

Successful revolutions are the ones that mobilize not just a niche group of activists but large and diverse swaths of a population. As Robert H. Dix argued in his seminal essay, "Why Revolutions Succeed & Fail," "More than any particular socioeconomic level which may be said to make a polity ripe for revolutionary change, a movement's

107 Garrett Gunderson, "Managing Change and Business Disruption Post-COVID," *Forbes*, August 22, 2020, https://www.forbes.com/sites/garrettgunderson/2020/08/22/managing-change-and-business-disruption-post-covid/.

108 "If You Want Your Digital Transformation to Succeed, Align Your Operating Model to Your Strategy," *Harvard Business Review*, January 31, 2020, https://hbr.org/sponsored/2020/01/if-you-want-your-digital-transformation-to-succeed-align-your-operating-model-to-your-strategy.

109 Gunderson.

ability to assemble a broad 'negative' coalition of diverse domestic groups and foreign supporters, including elite groups and the middle class, may be essential for success."[110]

Change doesn't work unless everybody is doing it. In an organization, that means looking at all the different project stakeholders. You have your senior leaders. You have your HR; often, it's the HR VPs who are running communication throughout the organization. You have your manager group. And you have your individual employees. All of these stakeholders have to get on board.

Typically, when organizations implement Fuel50's software, there's at least one stakeholder who is really passionate about this change initiative—passionate enough to have gotten us into the organization. Our first step, always, is cultivating the passion of the other stakeholders so that they also take ownership of the project.

Organizations tend not to take the time to do the groundwork of engaging stakeholders that would really help them over time—especially with an all-organization initiative. Often there's so many layers of decision-making that nothing gets solidified until the 11th hour. Then it's the night before the program is launching, and senior leadership is sending an email to their VP of HR asking them to complete all these tasks for a project they're not engaged with. Don't wait until the 11th hour to bring in your HR VPs and your manager group. Bring them in early; engage them in the process.

Effective change requires emotional awareness about people. Because ultimately, it's not organizational change; it's people change. If you just look at it as a plan on a piece of paper, you're missing out. At the end of the day, it's people that are effecting the transformation. People are going to either support or not support the change. That

110   Robert H. Dix, "Why Revolutions Succeed & Fail," *Polity* 16, no. 3 (March 1, 1984): 423–46, https://doi.org/10.2307/3234558.

extra layer of intention and consideration, of cultivating ownership among all stakeholders at all levels, is missing.

A good revolutionary leader asks, "What is your role in this mission? How do you want to come along on this?" A revolution only works if everyone comes together. There has to be a collective consciousness around the movement. Over the past decade, organizations have started to make the shift toward being more cause driven, toward sharing their missions and creating a company culture in which everyone is aligned with and engaged by the company's mission. When it comes to organization-wide change and transformation, this buy-in is absolutely vital, for all stakeholder groups.

MANAGERS

When we work with clients to effect change, one of the focus points is always the manager group. Everybody has a natural resistance to change, but managers tend to be the most resistant to organizational change. Why? Because they didn't make the decision, but they have to effect it through their people.

When Fuel50 rolled out with Dexcom, we had all of the C-suite support we needed. The change we were trying to effect was a corporate goal. We had a big budget for a splashy rollout. Twenty-four hours after the rollout, we received an email from an employee saying, "I went in to do my reflection activities, and my manager looked at me as though I was wasting time and should be working."

This is why we come from a human-centered design perspective and streamline the messaging so it resonates with managers. We spend a lot of time talking to the manager population to answer the question, "What's in it for me?"

Bring managers into a focus group and ask what their pain points are and how leadership can help solve them. Even if you already know what the software or program can deliver, just asking the question will engage those stakeholders so much more in the solution.

SENIOR LEADERS

Often, even though it is the senior leaders who are implementing the change initiative, their mentality is, "This is for them, for the employees. This is not for me; I don't need it."

If an organization can get their senior leaders, their CEO, CFO, CMO, to also do the reflection exercises, to play around with the tool, to find value and get insight, it will help the transformation actually come to fruition. It doesn't matter what your title is or your level in the organization. There is always more to learn, always ways to transform and improve.

There is often a hesitancy among people in more junior roles to truly ask anything of their senior leaders. People assume senior leaders have no time. And yes, senior leaders are often very busy. But it never hurts to ask—and most of the time, you won't be rebuffed. Ask senior leaders to complete the reflection activities or shoot a couple videos talking about their values.

If leadership is talking a big talk about change, they need to actually believe in it, believe in the why, and stick with it. They can't just talk the talk; they have to walk the walk.

A recent article by McKinsey & Company underlines the importance of setting the tone at the top:

> In a McKinsey Global Survey conducted during the pandemic, just 43 percent of all respondents reported a positive team climate, the most important driver of psychological safety. Addressing this starts at the very top of an organization. By setting the tone through their own actions,

leaders have the strongest influence on psychological safety. Three key leader behaviors are:

- **Consultative**: Solicit input from team members and consider team views on issues that affect them.

- **Supportive**: Demonstrate concern and support for team members not only as employees but also as individuals.

- **Challenging**: Ask team members to reexamine assumptions about their work and how they can exceed expectations and fulfill their potential.

Senior leaders can act as catalysts, empowering and enabling others by role modeling and reinforcing behaviors they expect from the rest of the team.[111]

If you can get leadership aligned around the fact that there's a business reason for transforming your talent experience, the shift will be much easier. And it shouldn't be that difficult; after all, you want to keep people. Creating internal talent mobility can save you a lot of money. You'll be more productive, there will be more institutional knowledge, and you create more opportunities for others if you promote people internally. There's a huge amount of payoff for creating that change in an organization.

If leadership prioritizes development, it gives everybody else in the organization permission to prioritize their development as well. If an organization can get its senior leaders to have some humility and commit themselves to the change as well, it will help unify the organization. Leaders need to lead by example.

---

111   Aaron De Smet, Kim Rubenstein, and Kim Vierow, "Promoting Psychological Safety Starts with Developing Leaders," McKinsey & Company, May 24, 2021, https://www.mckinsey.com/business-functions/organization/our-insights/the-organization-blog/promoting-psychological-safety-starts-with-developing-leaders.

A Clear Message

Communication is the key to rallying people behind a vision. Perhaps there is no greater example of the power of communication in creating a revolution than Martin Luther King Jr.'s leadership of the Civil Rights Movement in the United States in the 1960s. Through his letters and, most famously, his speeches, King drew hundreds of thousands of people to marches across the country, most notably the March on Washington in 1963.

In his letters and speeches, King painted a clear, inspiring vision of a better future. Using plain language that everyone could relate to and understand—no political jargon or complicated rhetoric—he focused on a single *why*, a single, clear, coherent vision: equality for all races.

Clear, consistent messaging is essential to any movement for change. It's great to say, "This is unacceptable. This needs to change." But what does a successful outcome look like? It is vital to ground the whole organization in the big-picture goals. You have to think about the end state. Imagine you successfully effected the change you want. What does it look like? How do people relate to each other differently? How do people connect in a different way around talent?

Many times, the messaging gets lost in the noise of an hour-long presentation on the change initiative. This is why, when we roll out Fuel50, we always try to clarify a couple of key objectives.

Generally, people default to the assumption that people are smart and intuitive and can figure it out for themselves. And this is all true—but people are also really busy. So when we don't give them enough information, when we don't give them actionable steps and set aside time to complete those steps, they often simply don't have the brain space to focus on figuring out what to do. How can you serve it up in the most clear, simple, actionable way?

It might feel juvenile or patronizing to do this, but it's actually what people want. It means they don't have to use up their energy figuring out what you're asking them to do.

Clear communication for all stakeholders is vital. For every stakeholder, you need to say: here's the timeline for what we've agreed to do. Here is your role and the expectations we have of you. Each stakeholder group needs to be clear on the expectations and be willing to engage. Therefore, really simplistic, visual, streamlined communication and support tools are incredibly important: so no one has to wade through the noise.

The brain needs an A to Z. You can't just give someone B, F, K, P. You need a clear, simple, actionable message that people can remember. You need something someone can glance at and know what they are supposed to do—for example, a simple, high-level visual they can hang up next to their computer at their desk, illustrating the working norms for how the change will be executed.

Additionally, think about how the message can be communicated beyond just presentations and emails. How can you help people really connect with the message, raise their awareness, to get them the information in a way that will stick with them and motivate them?

It requires thinking outside the box—and also leveraging your greatest resource: the people around you.

Cultivating Ownership

Traditionally, we think of the people in the HR department as the experts. They're the ones tasked with pushing change information out to the organization. But with the internet, anybody can be an expert.

Anyone can look up change models and principles. HR doesn't have to be the only people generating content.

Instead of HR simply pushing out informational content, HR can curate and facilitate content as well. Perhaps HR sets up an internal video channel, and encourages employees to interview each other about their careers and development and share those stories on the channel. You can have engagement champions who help that work. You can have early adopters become influencers, leveraging their creativity to make the change initiative part of company culture.

Who across your organization has a vision or ideas around people practices? Maybe that person leads the revolution in your organization. Maybe it's not somebody in HR but a charismatic person in another department who can see a better way across the organization and who can champion that vision.

This is precisely what happened at Gore-Tex. Gore-Tex famously has a flat organizational structure, with not a single manager among the 10,000 employees. They have no leader culture; instead, everybody is a contributor. However, there are occasional leaders either temporarily or more permanently who are defined and chosen by their "followship." As Debra France of W. L. Gore & Associates (Gore-Tex's parent company) describes it,

> When looking for someone to lead the People Function, it was put to the entire business: who would you follow in this organization in relation to People Leading practices? Who is doing things in the People space that you admire and who are making a difference in the way they work? From the employees' responses, a "leader" is identified.... We do have leaders, and those leaders are defined by follwership.

In other words—you are a leader when other people want to follow you.[112]

It didn't matter whether the person had a degree in HR or whether they had "moved up the ladder" to a leadership position. The leader was selected from the people, by the people, giving everyone a sense of ownership over the role.

Sometimes, HR gets in their own way by thinking they know better than everyone else. They're not really open to cultivating the brilliance of others. They don't open their eyes to what other people in the organization may have to offer a change movement. But a revolution requires engagement and ownership and will have a much greater chance of success if *everyone's* brilliance can be incorporated. "Rearrange the letters in the word 'listen,' and you get 'silent,'" Richard Branson points out in his book *The Virgin Way*. "The only way to listen to the other person is to be silent, without interrupting them or planning what you want to say before they're done."[113]

When forming the UWF, Cesar Chavez and Dolores Huerta didn't merely bring together a diverse coalition; they listened to everyone and made them a part of the process, as Matt Garcia notes:

> Chavez achieved his early success through a combination of political savvy and attentiveness to workers' concerns.... This outreach, as his mentor Fred Ross had taught him, required a tremendous amount of patience and listening. Rather than push a solution upon communities in need, Ross encouraged members to meet, argue, and eventually come to collective decisions. Strategically deployed, such demo-

---

112 Anne Fulton, *The Career Engagement Game: Shaping Careers for an Agile Workforce* (Auckland: Fuel50, 2014).

113 Richard Branson, *The Virgin Way: How to Listen, Learn, Laugh and Lead,* Virgin Digital, 2014.

cratic methods gave participants a sense of ownership over the goals of the movement and inspired deeper investments among its adherents. Chavez urged organizers to be creative in their tactics, which enabled many volunteers to discover new methods for achieving their goals. The nimbleness and independence that Chavez encouraged among his organizers led to a union with deeper roots and more effective strategies than any of its predecessors had achieved.[114]

The Voice of the People

While many revolutions and change movements are led by a charismatic, visionary leader, in recent years we have also seen incredible, world-changing movements, such as the Black Lives Matter and #MeToo movements, without a single visible leader. In fact, the Black Lives Matter movement became the biggest civil rights movement in history without a Gandhi or a Che Guevara or a Martin Luther King Jr.

At the beginning of July 2020, the *New York Times* reported that

Four recent polls—including one released this week by Civis Analytics, a data science firm that works with businesses and Democratic campaigns—suggest that about 15 million to 26 million people in the United States have participated in demonstrations over the death of George Floyd and others in recent weeks. These figures would make the recent protests

114 Garcia.

the largest movement in the country's history, according to interviews with scholars and crowd-counting experts.[115]

And the protests weren't limited to the United States; all across the world, massive protests against racial injustice sprang up. How did this enormous national and international uprising happen in such a short time—and without a single charismatic leader leading the charge? Many factors were at play, but one, cited by the *New York Times*, was the rapid availability of information. There was, of course, the horrifying video of George Floyd's murder, which went viral on the internet. And it was also online that the movement grew and spread:

> One of the reasons there have been protests in so many places in the United States is the backing of organizations like Black Lives Matter. While the group isn't necessarily directing each protest, it provides materials, guidance and a framework for new activists, [Deva Woodly, an associate professor of politics at the New School] said. Those activists are taking to social media to quickly share protest details to a wide audience.[116]

This is very different from revolutions of the past—and it's a change that is reflected in the workplace. In an article on change management trends to look out for in 2021, Changefirst underlines that "real-time data will be a key asset for change management." The fast data we have today allows us to check the pulse of what's happening, to hear the voice of the people in real time.

115   Larry Buchanan, Quoctrung Bui, and Jugal K. Patel, "Black Lives Matter May Be the Largest Movement in U.S. History," *New York Times*, July 3, 2020, sec. U.S., https://www.nytimes.com/interactive/2020/07/03/us/george-floyd-protests-crowd-size.html.

116   Ibid.

The voice of the people is what made the #MeToo and Black Lives Matter movements so powerful. One thing that has become clear—especially in movements like the #MeToo movement and the Black Lives Matter movement—is that the people need a voice. Organizations need to listen more carefully and create an opportunity for employee voices to be heard, for employees to be empowered. And the organizations we have worked with where change has been effective are the organizations that have created a voice for their people and have listened to that voice.

The voice of the people in organizations today says that our talent practices have to be different. You ignore that voice at your peril.

Persistence and Commitment

Revolutions may spring into being as swiftly as a spark lighting a forest fire, but they don't succeed overnight. The #MeToo and Black Lives Matter movements, while they each had their moments in the limelight, have been working for many, many years to effect change. Martin Luther King Jr. didn't give one brilliant speech and call it a day; he spoke and wrote and marched and led for years before his assassination. Mahatma Gandhi didn't lead India to independence from Britain in a day. Revolutions succeed because people rally to a vision of a better future—and then *stick with that vision*, however long it takes.

One common reason change initiatives fail is because organizations deprioritize them. The change initiative is shiny and splashy and new when it launches. Most organizations will take the time to do the launch, to get the software and programming out there. Then they move on to something else. Six months later, the project team that put it into place has moved on to something else shiny and new, and the change initiative is left languishing.

Organizations are barges, not speedboats. Change takes time and dedication. Transformation initiatives can't be a fad, a fashion, a flash in the pan. It's not a few weeks or even a few months that are needed for change; it's really the next one, two, or three years that are going to define the success of the initiative. Too often, organizations don't have the patience to do it. So they end up staying status quo, and the flashy, trendy change initiative they rolled out never comes to fruition, never reaches its full potential. Organizations lose out on creating real change because they commit to something, then they shift to something else.

Organizations are barges, not speedboats. Change takes time and dedication. Transformation initiatives can't be a fad, a fashion, a flash in the pan.

It's very easy for a change initiative to become out of sight, out of mind. It's easy to deprioritize, because other, more urgent matters arise. This is why it's critical to understand the difference between "urgent" and "important."

Here's an analogous example: you wake up every day with the intention of working out. Then you get busy with work—there are so many urgent matters to attend to. By the end of the day, after a full day of attending to these urgent matters, you are so tired that you don't work out. You prioritized the urgent things—work matters—but you didn't prioritize the *important* thing: your health. A day or two may not make a difference, but over time, prioritizing the urgent over the important will have a negative effect. Then it will demand your attention, and it will be a lot harder to address and take care of.

If you really want to shift organizational culture, if you want to make sure the *important* doesn't get subsumed by the *urgent*, you have to commit and reinforce the structure that allows people to actually lean into and effect change. Create a culture across the organization in which everybody is focused on the change initiative, on their development.

Some organizations do things like "Development Tuesdays," when employees are free to pursue development opportunities. Some organizations have spaces within their corporate offices that function as development hubs, where people can get away from their desk, shift gears a little bit, and focus on their development for a bit of time.

It's not just about the tools and features of the program or platform; it's also about how you can take those things off-line. Can people do value exercises and share them with their manager and teammates? Can managers facilitate those conversations? Find the connection points to take some of the work off-line. Embed it into the talent ecosystem so that it becomes part of the way people connect to each other.

In order to make sure these structures are adhered to, every stakeholder needs to have accountability around executing the change process. How do you hold people accountable in a meaningful way? Too often, holding people accountable goes out the window. People just step over things they should be calling out, because nobody wants to create interpersonal tension.

That's why it's important to create spaces for accountability based in vulnerability and trust, where there is an agreement that everyone stays in a space of positive intent. Unfortunately, this rarely happens. It is frequently the missing link in actually effecting change.

All of this takes a lot of work. Stick with your plan. Don't give up and change course. Creating a culture shift takes a lot of energy, effort, and teamwork, with everyone focused on the same direction over time. And it will only be effective if managers and leaders—especially at a high level—take all the steps as well. As the *Forbes* article cited earlier states, "We all need to feel like we're rowing in the same direction, that we're in this together, and that leadership is right there rowing with us."[117]

Put All the Pieces Together

There are many different elements that make a revolution successful, and there are many different strategies for achieving that success. But the most successful revolutions don't just encompass one element or one strategy. Successful revolutions engage from multiple angles, at multiple levels. They engage politically, through legislation, and at street level, through protests, marches, and grassroots organizing. They have visionary leaders, and they engage and listen to the voice of the people, giving the people ownership over the movement. They have attention-grabbing events and rollouts, and they have years of structured groundwork preceding and following those events.

As Mark and Paul Engler, coauthors of *This Is an Uprising: How Nonviolent Revolt Is Shaping the Twenty-First Century*, argue, it was not a single strategy that allowed Mahatma Gandhi to lead India to independence from the British. "In truth," they write, "it was not one strategy, but the combination of several. And a large part of the political genius of Mohandas Gandhi lay in his ability to bring these disparate strategies together." Gandhi, they write, used three strategies that are still present in social movements today: large-scale mobilizations that employ nonviolent direct action, efforts to build lasting

---

117 Gunderson.

organizational structure, and the creation of alternatives outside the mainstream.

The Englers write that combining strategies is also the best option for today's revolutionary movements:

> Some people work to create mass mobilizations—actions such as the Women's March, Occupy Wall Street, or large immigrant rights protests—that draw significant public attention but that can fade away quickly. Others focus on the slow-and-steady work of building long-term institutions, such as unions or political parties. Still other groups foster countercultural communities and alternative institutions outside of the mainstream. Often, there is little contact between groups employing different strategies—and little sense of common purpose.

> However, these different efforts need not see themselves at odds with one another. Movements function best when they recognize diverse roles and find ways to employ the contributions of each in constructive ways. In fact, this can be a key to success.[118]

We are at a moment in history when the ground is fertile for revolution. The pandemic disrupted so much of the way we work; armed with these lessons from successful revolutions, we can take this moment of transformation and create a blueprint for the change we want to see in talent management.

---

118   Mark Engler and Paul Engler, "Gandhi's Strategy for Success—Use More than One Strategy," *Waging Nonviolence* (blog), March 17, 2017, https://wagingnonviolence.org/2017/03/gandhi-strategy-success/.

CUSTOMER JOURNEYS THROUGH CHANGE

Case Study F

> **Organization: A multinational pharmaceutical corporation based in Europe. One of the largest pharmaceutical companies in the world, employing 110,000 people worldwide.**

THE VISION

A brand-new talent marketplace should enable open access for everyone to drive their careers in an unbossed world. We reimagine career development as a democratic, transparent, and agile experience that applies technology and data to match talent supply to business demand, install a state-of-the-art talent marketplace software solution, redefine talent processes, and instill a new mindset on talent brokering, development, and careers, thereby fueling our cultural transformation.

Key Benefits Include:

- Democratizes career development

- Facilitates and accelerates talent exchange

- Improves employee experience

- Increases talent visibility

- Supports associate career exploration

- Digitizes and introduces AI to talent practices

- Keeps pace with the dynamic, changing talents needs of the business

- Enables distributed working, including virtual assignments

- All-encompassing platform for all opportunities, including jobs, gigs, etc.

- Enables mentoring matches

- Directs associates to key learning offerings to close possible gaps

- Creates easy access to data for insights and informed decision-making

- Consolidates technology footprint (Workday, LXP, etc.)

Case Study G

Organization: British multinational banking and financial services company, headquartered in London, England, operating a network across more than 70 countries and employing around 87,000 people.

This organization is in the third year of an HR transformation executing to a highly developed HR and talent strategy.

The people strategy consists of the following elements:

1. Shape and enable a client-centric and adaptable organization.

2. Develop and deploy the right talent (skills and capabilities) in the areas of biggest opportunity.

3. Create an inclusive culture that leverages our diversity to deliver prosperity for our clients and communities.

4. Build a future-ready workforce.

If achieved well, each progressed ambition will have a positive roll on effect to other ambitions.

The problems we are trying to solve for are as follows:

- How might we improve our people's perceptions of career, growth, and development opportunities on offer in the bank?

- How can we accelerate our ability to help our people upskill and reskill to build a future-ready workforce?

- How might we make it easy to locate, connect, and deploy people who have the skills needed in areas of the biggest opportunity?

- How might we unlock workforce productivity with new approaches to developing and deploying talent?

- How might we create an inclusive, transparent, and open approach to showcasing career and development opportunities on offer?

- How might we enable people to get insight into how they can manage their own careers and progression in the future world of work?

CHAPTER 6

A Blueprint for Change

After three months of reading and learning, Liberty began to codify and itemize what she had learned across all the dimensions she had explored: what she learned from her observations, what she learned from the voice of her people and all their different perspectives, and what she learned from reading about those who had created change in history—for better or for worse.

Then she decided she needed to write down her own principles—a charter for what she believed would be a better world. This world would be based on fairness of opportunity, on leveraging the individual and collective talents of those around her, on knowledge and skill sharing—including the need to create a mechanism for sharing knowledge, skills, and talents for the collective good of her community.

Everyone had a role to play in creating this new world. Even the children could contribute. And it would operate in a democratic style, with the community choosing who to follow based on who showed the best leadership.

While the coronavirus pandemic created innumerable challenges for organizations and individual employees, it has also cracked open new possibilities. As Jason Lauritsen, an author, advisor, leadership trainer, and workplace culture expert based in Omaha, Nebraska, recently wrote,

> There has been more disruption to the way work gets done in the past few months than in the previous decade. This virus forced us to cut through bureaucracy, red tape, and old school management practices to find a way to survive.
>
> And yet, both Gallup and Quantum Workplace have reported data that shows a dramatic improvement in employee engagement trends during the pandemic when compared to past years.
>
> What do we really know for sure at this point?... We know that employees are far more resilient, resourceful, and committed to their jobs than most organizations assumed.
>
> We (also) know that when we are properly motivated, we can get things done and make things happen, even big complex things, a lot faster than we thought. Our slow, political, bureaucratic processes have been like anchors holding us

in place. The bigger your organization, the heavier that anchor.[119]

Yes, people have the innate ability to be flexible and agile, but as Lauritsen observed, they can take those natural abilities to higher levels when they are motivated to do so. A sudden transformational event like a worldwide pandemic can ignite that motivation; the *Harvard Business Review* makes the case too, arguing that "there's nothing like a crisis to ignite innovation.... [And] the current pandemic has already led to countless innovations."[120]

How has that happened? Agility is the key. In the pandemic, this was often agility on the fly, a rapid response to a sudden organizational challenge that demanded quick action. As the *Harvard Business Review* describes it: "Typically, a small group of people spotted an urgent need, dropped lower-priority activities, broke typical bureaucratic procedures, and transformed from everyday workers to real-life corporate MacGyvers, surprising themselves and their bosses in the process."

However, they add that agility that occurs as a response mechanism does not always take root with employees or their organizations. "This spur-of-the-moment agility is fragile," they note. "Innovations happen sporadically rather than systematically. And when the emergency fades, people typically return to traditional command-and-control innovation until the next crisis arises, when they must reinvent agile approaches all over again."[121]

---

119   Jason Lauritsen, "No. The Future of Work Is *Not* Work from Home,"
        Jason Lauritsen, August 21, 2020, https://jasonlauritsen.com/2020/08/
        no-the-future-of-work-is-not-work-from-home/.

120   Darrell K. Rigby, Sarah Elk, and Steve Berez, "Develop Agility That Outlasts the
        Pandemic," *Harvard Business Review*, May 15, 2020, https://hbr.org/2020/05/
        develop-agility-that-outlasts-the-pandemic.

121   Ibid.

This begs the question: How can workforce agility and flexibility drive meaningful (and lasting) workplace innovations for both employees *and* their organizations?

> **Organizations who are fair, transparent, inclusive, and respectful of their people are the ones who will thrive into the future.**

Organizations who are fair, transparent, inclusive, and respectful of their people are the ones who will thrive into the future. We need a more human/humane work experience, and the time is here. Talent practices will be better than they were last decade: more human, more people centric, more intelligent, more robust in their skills and capability matching, more learning and growth oriented, more enabling, and better able to deliver the talent optimization that organizations will need in the coming decade. The time for this new era in the talent experience and talent enablement is here.

The Psychology Behind Talent Mobility

As organizations consolidate their resources because of the COVID-19 pandemic, it has become increasingly important to do more with less. With furloughing and hiring freezes currently commonplace, many businesses have started looking inward to identify how best to use the talent already at their disposal.

Equally, the shift to remote working has accelerated digital transformation plans that have been in the pipeline for years. As workers have been asked to rapidly adapt to new circumstances and technologies, the conversations around employee engagement and reskilling the workforce have moved to the forefront.

Against such a backdrop, getting internal mobility right has arguably never been more important.

Internal talent mobility is the process of moving people within your workforce to fill open opportunities. This can include promotions to new roles, short-term redeployment, gig opportunities, or moves to different departments. At its core, internal talent mobility is a strategy that enables organizations to nurture and retain key talent by matching employees with internal opportunities in which they can optimize their skill sets, helping both the employee and the business grow.

Benefits of such a strategy are vast, but perhaps the most important is double sided: internal mobility improves employee engagement and, in the process, grows the bottom line.

EMPLOYEE ENGAGEMENT

What we are seeing is that internal mobility, career development, and career growth are all absolutely in demand right now. People are willing to learn more within their current organization and even their current role. People want to move their careers forward and are actively looking to grow and develop.

Smart, forward-thinking organizations will focus on prioritizing the demand for development and growth and will work to implement a new set of norms that both enable and encourage internal talent mobility. Those that do this will be far more likely to thrive in this new world of work.

According to aggregate agility data compiled by Fuel50,

- **22% of people are willing to be moderately mobile and flexible** in where they work and may be open to considering locations beyond their current place of work.

- **36.6% of people are keen to accelerate** and fast-track their careers.

- **28.6% of people are willing to grow** their careers.

- **21.2% of people feel they have a lot more to learn** in their careers.

- **21.1% of people are looking for learning and development** opportunities within their current role.

THE BUSINESS CASE FOR INTERNAL MOBILITY

Leveraging your existing talent can be a great way to build organizational and personal resilience—while maintaining productivity and saving money, time, and resources. Internal mobility not only engages staff and retains top talent; it also gets the best from an organization's workforce without time-consuming and costly external recruitment, as these statistics show:

- Compared with internal hires in similar positions, external hires are 61% more likely to be laid off or fired in their first year of service and 21% more likely to leave.[122]

---

122   Robin Erickson, Denise Moulton, and Bill Cleary, "Are You Overlooking Your Greatest Source of Talent?" Deloitte Insights, July 30, 2018, https://www2.deloitte.com/us/en/insights/deloitte-review/issue-23/unlocking-hidden-talent-internal-mobility.html.

- It can cost six times less to build talent from within than to hire externally.[123]

- 87% of employers agreed an internal mobility program would help their retention goals.[124]

- 87% of employers agreed an internal mobility program would help attract better talent.[125]

WHERE TO START

Ascertaining the lay of the land is critical. Human resources directors should review existing internal talent mobility programs, starting with the elements that have worked previously, and identifying those that require an overhaul.

As part of this review, HR professionals must consider how well they know their workforce. What are their employees' skills and strengths? How do they perform? Which elements of their role do they most value and why? What are their career aspirations?

The effectiveness of internal mobility technology is determined by the accuracy of this employee information, so it is imperative HR leaders support line managers in gathering as much qualitative data as possible about their team members' skill sets and job requirements, as well as future career goals.

This data can be gathered through multiple touchpoints, including employee surveys, regular virtual check-ins between managers and employees, and via job portals, all of which can uncover vital insights

---

123   Josh Bersin, "Build vs. Buy: The Days of Hiring Scarce Technical Skills Are Over," Josh Bersin, October 23, 2019, https://joshbersin.com/2019/10/build-vs-buy-the-days-of-hiring-scarce-technical-skills-are-over/.

124   Erickson.

125   Ibid.

into workforce sentiment. These insights can help businesses better engage employees and tailor development opportunities.

Internal mobility is an ideal avenue through which to engage and retain talent, granting access to new opportunities across job roles, projects, programs, and short-term gigs, which is vital during the current period of disruption and rapid change.

INSIDE FIRST

We have a responsibility to our people to look internally before externally. The labor market forces are so tough out there right now that we have to ensure we have given opportunities within our existing workforce to match to our employment contracts and psychological contracts by providing opportunities to leverage existing capability within our business first.

The best revolutions start with us. We have an abundant talent supply, but our first responsibility is to our people within our organization. So look internally. Before we go looking at the external recruitment talent supply, we have a responsibility to make sure our own people are getting opportunities. We must be more about the people for whom we are responsible. They're part of our workforce.

Inclusive and Diverse

Inclusivity is the burning imperative right now. The pandemic era combined with the global activism ignited by the Black Lives Matter movement means inclusivity and diversity are at the forefront for every organization we talk to today.

This is a reminder to organizations that all employees, irrespective of who they are or where they come from, must be treated equally. We are at a point in history where the world is united against the mistreatment of people in our communities because of the color of their skin (or anything else for that matter). The world of work needs to respond quickly to ensure all people feel included and are treated equally and fairly. We anticipate that organizations' processes and policies will be subjected to scrutiny to ensure this. Organizations may be affected by "employee walkouts" if it is not achieved.

Inclusivity, diversity, culture, and values are paramount to workforce infrastructure. It is essential to create a level playing field for employees where *everyone* has a clear line of sight to opportunities and growth. In the past, there has been little to no transparency around openings and opportunities within an organization, and many suitable employees never had the opportunity to be considered for projects or roles.

This is one of the imperatives behind the work we do at Fuel50. Our platform aims to remove this bias and create transparency for fairness and inclusivity through an AI-driven, open talent marketplace, with insights that support leaders to make decisions based on best talent fit. Through good-quality data, talent can be placed on a level playing field. Talent-decision transparency creates fair organizations.

In a world where all people need to feel included and treated equally, the main element driving business talent strategies going forward is capability. Organizations need to become more capable by making talent decisions that are not only transparent and fair, but that also give *everyone* a clearer view of their future. Now, more than ever, this is a top-of-mind concern for workers everywhere.

Transparent and Democratic

Transparency will drive fairness and inclusivity. If *all* opportunities are open to all people across our business, then we can be more fair and inclusive to all. Transparency gives everyone an equal opportunity to participate and have their voice heard.

Moreover, the transparency around employees' personal skills will allow matching to opportunities—both vacancies and, more importantly, projects, gigs, stretch assignments, and experiences, which historically have been even less transparent than vacancies.

That's why the next frontier in transparency is the experience marketplace, where all opportunities are visible, and employees can understand what skills they need to invest in to seize those opportunities and create even more opportunities for their future.

Unlocking hidden talent within your organization requires transparency to the skills and capabilities that your people currently possess, as well as those they are willing to grow and develop. Equip your leaders to drive this transformation and manage talent in a whole new way. Train your leaders to have powerful career development conversations that seek out the values, talents, and ambitions of employees, and work to find ways to satisfy those aspirations.

Information is power, so set up a database where managers can input information on the values, talents, and ambitions of employees. Give leaders across the business access to search, discover, and tap into talent that might be suitable for open opportunities. Power up HR, business partners, and chief people officers to be able to have the data they need to take to their stakeholders around the capability gaps, succession risks, and reskilling momentum across the business.

Employers need to assess the ease with which existing employees can change jobs and find other opportunities within their organization. For example, where can they find information about relevant opportunities within the business? Who are the key points of contact for each role? What is the process for applying for a new opportunity?

"Rather than automatically opening a job requisition when a manager needs a role filled, it's time to think about how organizations can continuously access talent in varying ways: mobilizing internal resources, finding people in the alternative workforce, and strategically leveraging technology to augment sourcing and boost recruiting productivity," explains the *2019 Deloitte Global Human Capital Trends Report.*[126]

The report cites Trane Technologies (formerly known as Ingersoll Rand) as a business doing things right: "Trane Technologies, for example, developed a robust internal career program to help employees reskill themselves for new positions within the organization, and invested in an interactive, analytics-based technology solution that allows them to explore and access alternative roles and career paths across the company. The result: a nearly 30 percent increase in employee engagement." Trane also saw big shifts in their internal to external recruitment ratios with internal placements increasing from 35% to 55% of positions filled internally, within two years of deploying the talent marketplace.

A platform like Fuel50's creates this kind of transparent information sharing through customizable features, allowing organizations to easily access their talent and see who has the skills, and who is developing those skills, to get the right people into the right job or project in accordance with business demands. The gig network and cross-function talent-sharing will help enterprise businesses fill key talent gaps while growing their employees' careers. Mentoring is a great way to support cross-organizational career development, help

---

126   *2019 Deloitte Global Human Capital Trends*, Deloitte Insights, 2019, https://www2. deloitte.com/content/dam/Deloitte/cz/Documents/human-capital/cz-hc-trends-reinvent-with-human-focus.pdf.

others fulfill and fast-track their high potentials, build networks, and gain critical experience and skills needed for new opportunities.

This kind of transparency helps organizations guide people to the jobs of the future, enable their crew to continually reskill and upskill, and provide visibility for future roles within the organization. It enables organizations to align their business requirements and organizational strategies more closely, give employees a clearer visual into their future career paths within the company, and future-proof the organization with greater workforce agility along the way.

ETHICAL AI

While an AI platform like Fuel50's is an invaluable tool, more than ever we need to take care how we are using AI when it comes to people decisions. Is historical data perpetuating some old-code ways or built-in biases? We need to carefully examine our paradigms and lenses on talent to ensure we are supporting important business fundamentals and values. We must put aside the historic and look at the blueprint. Who is writing the code? Are they all from a single demographic? How diverse is the team creating the AI and algorithms? Are the code writers thinking about the impact of the code on the people on the receiving end?

Using historical data has lots of risk for your inclusivity and diversity imperatives. For example, say the last five people who went into a particular position were all white men in their 50s who had MBAs from Ivy League schools and a certain number of years in particular management roles. A standard AI system would automatically take that bio data and rate those characteristics as top priority when matching people with that role. Those middle-aged white men would be the blueprint in the system for that opportunity—meaning the AI would potentially automatically mark, say, a woman of color with a degree from a state university as a lower match for the job.

Therefore, when working with AI, we need to be very careful that the matching science is supporting the organization's broader goals around inclusivity. Without oversight, AI could create an even more insular and exclusive talent culture.

But as we've discussed, used correctly and consciously, AI can throw wide the doors of opportunity, creating a more equitable talent marketplace for everyone. Say the AI tool shows that woman of color with a degree from a state school to have some talent gaps. Instead of saying, "You are not a good fit for this position," an inclusive marketplace would communicate, "You have these talents and this potential, and maybe some specific skill gaps. Let's now match you with the mentors, coaches, training, and experience you need. Here is a mentor you can work with; here are some classes you can take; here are some projects and stretch assignments you can work on to help you make this goal a reality." The goal is enablement rather than exclusion or rejection.

Self-Sustaining and People First

Sourcing talent internally along with growing and reskilling employees may require a cultural shift within your organization, especially if you've been concentrating on external recruitment. Long-term investments in an overall culture of talent development are key to building a culture of cross-team talent sharing and internal mobility.

Organizations have flattened. People are spending longer times in their roles. The jump to a next level opportunity is typically steeper and more complex. An organization may be really committed to internal mobility, but that can only happen if people are ready for those next-level roles. If people are not ready, the company will look externally to fill those roles. If an organization really wants to create those opportunities for their people, they have to encourage people to develop in place.

Support leaders to build and sustain a culture of talent sharing where employees across the business are encouraged, and even expected to, look internally for personal growth, skills development, and new roles or challenges. Promote learning opportunities. Talk to your people about lateral moves, gigs, and stretch assignments. Make it easy for employees to find learning resources and development opportunities that are relevant to the skills and capabilities they want to develop. Introduce mentoring, and enable your employees to easily find, access, and request mentorship at key stages of their career to improve your culture of user-driven talent development and growth.

And among all the employee development, make sure you don't forget about managers. Many managers struggle to develop their people in any kind of meaningful way. Developing employees requires a sophisticated skill set, and managers don't typically get much training in how to develop their employees.

When it comes to management, HR tends to pull a bait and switch on people. We say, "You're good at your job. You have these skills. So we are going to give you more responsibility to do more of what you're good at." Then when the person continues to do good work, we say, "Now have a couple of direct reports. Do work through them." Over time, the person starts doing less of the work they're good at and delegating more work through others. As they move up in an organization, they're doing less of the technical, functional work they had been doing and more managing people.

The problem is, we don't give people training on how to do that— on how to manage others, how to delegate, how to lead a team, or how to help their people develop. That is a totally different skill set than the skill set we promoted them for. So in order for employees to develop, ensure that their managers are given the support to develop as well.

We can drive sustainable change one person at a time if we can enable each and every employee to be at their best, growing their skills for their own future and that of the organization. With the right technology, it is possible to grow a groundswell of change. One client we worked with saw their employees complete over a million experiential learning hours in six months, along with 375,000 reskilling actions taken across a workforce of 100,000. Avalanches come from snowflakes; all these micromoments of reskilling can aggregate to transform an organization from the bottom up.

Humanistic and Connecting

In the pandemic, our personal and professional worlds merged overnight. Our work lives entered our homes, as we not only worked from home but brought our work colleagues into our houses via Zoom. This was challenging, of course, but it also was enlightening. It reminded us that we are all humans, with lives and responsibilities outside of work, full and rich and deserving of attention, understanding, and empathy.

No two people in the world have the same challenges. We need to personalize our talent practices and people experiences based on the circumstances of each individual in our organization. Technology can help us do this at scale.

Nothing creates more empathy and understanding than person-to-person connection. The collaborative and connective tissue into our talent practices has become more important as we have lost our water-cooler touchpoints, team drinks and off-site opportunities for connection. Although these opportunities are starting to return, it shows the importance of baking opportunities for peer-to-peer learning and connection into your talent practices. Connections such as finding a mentor or someone to ask questions of who is doing something you would like to learn needs to be embedded into your internal talent mobility systems and marketplace.

We also need to foster environments that are beneficial to the overall well-being of everyone in the organization.

HOW ORGANIZATIONS CAN INCREASE WELL-BEING

In our recent *Fuel50 Capability Trends Report*™, we examined wellness in the workplace and identified 15 of the latest globally trending capabilities associated with driving a wellness culture.[127]

As the *Fuel50 Capability Trends Report*™ notes:

The global pandemic has elevated [wellness] to a critical strategic priority for organizations globally. Governments, communities, and workplaces all need to do their bit to ensure people have support and resources to safeguard their wellness....

[R]esearch has shown that those organizations that invest in wellness have healthy employees who are more productive and less likely to be absent. In return, organizations gain on their health and wellness investments and keep healthcare costs to a minimum.

Offering a range of wellness programs is one tactic for lifting levels of employee well-being in an organization. However, we know

---

127 *Capability Trends Report: Workplace Wellness Edition*, Fuel50, 2021, https://www. fuel50.com/resources/capability-trends-report-2021-q2/.

that to create a culture with employee wellness at its heart, you need to consider and elevate specific employee capabilities and skills.

Belonging

One element of well-being is the concept of "belonging," as introduced in Deloitte's 2020 Human Capital Trends Survey. This is about employees craving a sense of belonging to something greater in these testing times. Their research found that to drive organizational success, 79% of respondents said creating a sense of belonging within the workplace was critical. To achieve this, organizations need to optimize the power of individuals by connecting them through their purpose at work.[128]

Open, transparent communication will help organizations and their people thrive. There is a greater need for communication, collaboration, openness, and trust than ever before, which is why we have seen demand for digital employee experience solutions surge in demand in the last year. The more chaos and change there is, the more people crave clarity and communication.

Our Crisis Change Response Journey

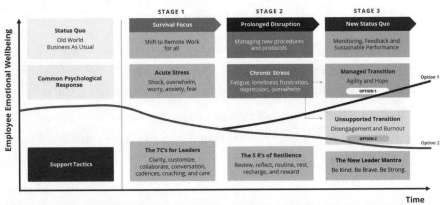

Source: Fuel50, Work-Fit Handbook 2020

128 "Deloitte Human Capital Trends Survey 2020," Deloitte, 2020, https://www2.deloitte.com/nz/en/footerlinks/pressreleasespage/2020-deloitte-human-capital-trends-survey.html.

Sleep First

Research by Deloitte also highlights the benefits of organizations creating an environment that "puts sleep first." With our "always on" culture, people's ability to learn, concentrate, and retain information is compromised because so many people are not well rested at work. Deloitte states that those organizations that devote resources to upskilling their employees on the benefits of sleep are reporting increased employee well-being, productivity, creativity, and innovation.[129]

Actions to encourage a well-rested workforce and sleep-first culture

Behavioral Nudges
- Commitment devices (e.g., sleep pledge)
- Reminders
- Social proof
- Storytelling

Rewards & Incentives
- Educational/developmental training
- Create programs that incentivize sleep

Environmental
- Natural light
- Nap rooms
- Beverage and food availability/accessibility

Technology/Policy
- Limit or disable after-hours emails
- Discourage or disable after-hours video calls

Source: Deloitte Analysis

The Bottom Line: It's about Encouraging a Supportive Culture

Everyone has experienced unique challenges during the pandemic. But while each story is different, the outcome seems to be universal. There is a groundswell for organizations to provide a supportive environment where personal or professional challenges are acknowledged and support is offered if needed.

---

129 Jen Fisher, Susan K. Hogan, and Amy Fields, "You Snooze, You Win," Deloitte Insights, February 4, 2019, https://www2.deloitte.com/content/www/global/en/insights/focus/behavioral-economics/sleep-benefits-impact-employee-performance.html.

Research conducted on behalf of SEEK found that "1 in 3 candidates who are thinking about changing careers are doing so for better work-life balance…. What's more, people are keenly aware of whether businesses are truly committed to offering flexibility, or whether they're just spouting empty words."

SEEK outlines nine key workplace factors from their research that matter most to employees and candidates: engagement; relationships ("1 in 2 people feel workplace relationships have become more important compared to pre-COVID, and more than half prefer a workplace where their colleagues are also their friends"); meaning and purpose ("2 in 3 candidates want a job that gives them an opportunity to make a difference to society"); support with goals; sense of achievement; true flexibility; trust; mental health support ("40% of candidates say they would have liked more mental health support during COVID-19, regardless of whether the workplaces have existing support in place or not"); and ongoing learning.[130]

It appears that the pendulum has swung, and organizations are doing what they can to encourage more supportive workplace cultures. And when that has happened, it has come by leaders pivoting and changing their organizational practices to provide employees what

> **There is a groundswell for organizations to provide a supportive environment where personal or professional challenges are acknowledged and support is offered if needed.**

---

130   Helen Tobler, "9 Things Employees Expect in a Workplace in 2021," SEEK Hiring Advice, February 2021, https://seek.co.nz/employer/hiring-advice/9-things-employees-expect-in-a-workplace-in-2021.

they want—increased levels of workplace communication, transparency, authenticity, resilience, and humanistic qualities.

Our Top Seven Tips for Leaders to Help their People Through Change

Communicate	Customize	Collaboration	Cadences	Conversations	Coaching	Care Packages
communicate communicate.	your approach.	will be different.	are more important.	While some people might be in overload, others might have time to think more strategically about their future.	Hone your coaching skills to maximize your impact. Even simple questions can be powerful:	Think across your team who might be in need, or into your community and create a difference. Find others with energy to do something and rally them. Make individual contributions small but powerfully aligning and engaging too!
You cannot over-communicate right now, even if it is to say I have no update yet.	Every team member has a different challenge right now.	Handshakes have been replaced with elbow bumps but we need to be creative and find solutions to allow for collaboration and input creatively right now.	With remote work and hybrid work becoming the new normal, increase your regular cadences to check in with your team.		*What are you working on?*	
During times of change, people hunger for clarity.	Empathize with theirs and tailor your tactics to meet their challenges.		Keeping everyone in the loop will help them to stay motivated!	Ask what their learning goals are now and encourage them to use the time strategically.	*How can we progress this?* *What roadblocks can we remove?* *How else can I support you to progress this?*	

Source: Fuel50, Work-Fit Handbook 2020

It Is Time for HR to Transform from Business Partners to Business Makers

When it comes to revolutionizing talent management within organizations, it goes without saying that HR professionals will be at the center of creating that change. So to the HR practitioners reading this book, that means it is time to step into a new vision of what HR can be.

Being an HR business maker is about making a mark, taking charge of the organization's strategic vision, and aligning human resource people, processes, and practices to ensure organizational success. It's about transforming HR's image by continuously upskilling the function to create more value and influence.

This forward-looking vision for becoming business makers doesn't end with just making HR strategic and getting a seat at the strategy table. It assumes HR already has a seat at the table and focuses on what HR will do with it.

Top Employers Institute and AIHR HR trends reports indicate what HR can focus more on in 2022 and beyond. [131]

Here are key focus areas for HR to add the most value to their organizations:

1. **Change management:** HR needs to prepare for multiple possible futures and be agile enough to deal with these changes.

2. **Diversity, equity, inclusion, and belonging (DEIB):** Not only has DEI become increasingly important over recent years, but a sense of belonging has become an additional area to focus on to create a work environment that is fit for the new era of work. As AIHR describes it, "Belonging at work adds to the DEI equation. On the one hand, it is about 'longing to be,' while on the other hand, it is about 'being for long,' representing an affective and a temporal dimension. Belonging in the workplace brings a shift towards psychological safety and real inclusion."

3. **Data analytics:** HR needs to translate analytical outcomes into actions so that data is used optimally. Being more data literate is what can set HR apart from the competition.

4. **Organizational culture:** HR needs to create a culture of connection, collaboration, and trust in a digital work environment.

5. **Owner of business transformation:** Transformation is becoming the new normal, and HR has a large set of tools that can add immense value to business renewal.

---

131 *HR Trends Report 2021*, Top Employers Institute, 2021, https://www.top-employers.com/en-ZA/insights/culture/hr-trends-report-2021/; *HR Trends Report 2022*, December 9, 2021, https://www.aihr.com/blog/hr-trends-report-2022/.

6. **Digital transformation:** Not only will technology continue to add value to both the employees and the organizations, but HR also now needs to focus more on using technology for the good. HR has the ethical responsibility to use technology responsibly.

7. **Better talent allocation through talent marketplaces:** This helps to connect the workforce within an organization/ business unit to internal career opportunities. What will be even more prevalent this year is HR being more conscious of the importance of (planned) skill development. Consequently, more and more organizations are looking into partnering up with their strategic partners to create common talent marketplaces.

These are all areas that will become pivotal for helping HR to move beyond lingering stereotypes.

WHAT ELSE CAN HR DO TO MOVE BEYOND NEGATIVE STEREOTYPES AND DRIVE THE TRANSFORMATION OF THE ROLE OF HR?

*   **Demonstrate to employees the broader HR role** and contribution to the organization. In particular, change management, strategic planning, diversity and inclusivity, data analytics, and digital transformation may be good focus areas to highlight.

*   **Be more innovative in acquiring talent** to create an engaging candidate experience and to invest in their organization's brand. In addition, leverage technology to automate HR processes to create capacity for partnering and strategic HR.

This ensures that tasks are streamlined and HR resources are reinvested.

- **Be more transparent** in their sharing of data from initiatives implemented at their organizations. In turn, this may help with employees trusting HR more.

- **Use different tactics to gather timely feedback** from employees to determine the cultural health of the organization or any trending concerns. The key is to deal with these concerns quickly before it becomes an irreversible problem. As AIHR puts it, "When done well, HR teams appear more proactive and responsive to business needs."

- **Build an agile workforce culture**. As mentioned in Fuel50's "How to Build an Agile Work Culture in Your Organization": "Agile work is a critical part of a larger concept—internal talent mobility. It is a source of critical talent, a competitive advantage, and a driver of growth. Not only does it engage your staff and help to retain top talent, but internal mobility also allows you to get the best from your organization's workforce without costly and time-consuming external recruitment.... When you promote internal talent mobility, you encourage cross-team talent sharing and cultivate a culture of learning and development."[132] With this growth mindset, employees are better able to embrace change with confidence.

- **Focus on employee well-being**. *Harvard Business Review* predicts that "Wellness will become the newest metric that

---

132 "How to Build an Agile Work Culture in Your Organization—Fuel50," August 12, 2021, https://www.fuel50.com/2021/08/how-to-build-an-agile-work-culture/.

companies use to understand their employees."[133] When a people-centric approach is used, HR is seen as more concerned for the human experience, and in turn this drives a vibrant and supportive wellness culture.

- **Focus on** human-centric leadership and compassionate management. Research done by Gallup concluded that trust, compassion, stability, and hope are the areas the followers need from their leader.[134] By taking a human-centric leadership approach, these four areas can be addressed, and the people experience within organizations can be transformed.

- **Remain up to date on new or emerging roles within HR** (such as remote practice leaders). Technology can be leveraged to streamline processes to create capacity for emerging roles and responsibilities.

- **Continuous personal development**—upskilling, reskilling, and ongoing learning for the HR team to be seen as a credible and knowledgeable function. Moreover, HR plays a key role to ensure that leaders have the capability and capacity to lead with the right skill set and behaviors.

Creating revolutionary change is a big undertaking. But the moment is ripe for this revolution. And if you are still here, reading this book, then I know you are just as committed to and passionate about the talent revolution as we are—and together, we can make it a reality.

---

133   Brian Kropp and Emily Rose McRae, "11 Trends That Will Shape Work in 2022 and Beyond," *Harvard Business Review*, January 13, 2022, https://hbr.org/2022/01/11-trends-that-will-shape-work-in-2022-and-beyond.

134   Jim Harter, "COVID-19: What Employees Need from Leadership Right Now," Gallup, March 23, 2020, https://www.gallup.com/workplace/297497/covid-employees-need-leaders-right.aspx.

CUSTOMER JOURNEYS THROUGH CHANGE

Case Study H

> **Organization: European-based multinational pharmaceutical and biotechnology company employing 75,000 employees globally.**

Our goal is to provide career development tools and resources for all employees. As we build a culture of lifelong learning, we are focused on offering colleagues a range of learning options that enable colleagues to learn through experience, exposure, and education. We fundamentally believe that talent technology is key to fostering learning and growth and can provide the insights to empower colleagues to have better career conversations with their line managers and advocates.

With this in mind, we are evaluating technology that will

- Make it easier for employees to access experience-based development opportunities through a development marketplace and

- Enhance career and development planning through better visualization and guidance on career pathing options.

Case Study I

Organization: Swiss American multinational manufacturing company, with products sold in over 180 countries, employing 70,000 employees globally.

RESKILLING IMPERATIVE

Through strategic workforce planning (SWP), we aim to move from reactive vacancy management to a predictive and integrated total workforce planning process, led by a SWP business and employee experience, that gives direction to our talent acquisition, talent management, learning and development, mobility, and retention approach. SWP will provide, through workforce analytics and scenario modeling, better visibility to make data-driven decisions. Moreover, it will improve our employee engagement by providing transparency in opportunities for growth and clarity on where development is needed.

OBJECTIVES:

- Collect and display capabilities of all employees

- Validate critical capabilities for critical roles

- Analyze the impact of future business challenges/model on roles and capabilities (one to five years)

- Understand the current internal and external supply of these critical skills and evaluate and define the demand requirements, giving clear visibility to the current and potential future skills gap

- Provide capability gap insights for critical roles and establish build, buy, borrow plans (24–36 months)

- Establish always-on matching of people and critical capabilities (internal mobility, open sourcing, staffing) through an excellent user experience

We will do this through the following:

- Setting up a simple mechanism to collect existing capabilities of employees

- Focusing on identifying and validating critical capabilities and critical roles

- Testing and experimenting with functions, regions and markets and learning from this

- Providing relevant workforce analytics and using data to make decisions

- Enabling us to collect and include business and technological trends from outside

- Establishing best-in-class practice in strategic workforce planning

- Providing technology and analytics bases that support best-in-class practice

CONCLUSION

The Revolution Begins

How do you create change?

It starts with belief. If there is one thing we can learn from the world's great advocates for change, it's that you must have a real, deep, connected belief. To effectively bring about real change, you have to connect to your beliefs, connect to your power, connect to your true purpose.

At the beginning of this book, I asked you to consider these questions, when you consider creating change in your organization:

- What are you willing to fight for?

- What are you willing to champion?

- What are your core beliefs?

- What are your nonnegotiables?

- What is the experience you want to create within your organization?

- What difference do you want to make?

- What mark or impact do you want to leave on your organization?

- What do you want to be remembered for within your organization?

- What do you want your legacy to be?

Now I'd like to ask you to take out a piece of paper and a pencil— or pull up a new document on your computer—and write down your answer to these questions. This will help you create a core articulation of your vision and your purpose when it comes to the change you want to make in your organization—a charter of the defined principles you want to deliver and adhere to. This charter will be a North Star that you can follow, that will allow you to lead with conviction and purpose.

If you are an HR practitioner, you've probably supported and assisted the leadership of your organization through this exact process: creating a charter outlining the powerful beliefs that underpin the strategic principles and values of the organization. This is usually HR practitioner 101 work: helping leadership articulate the core values and purpose for the business.

For the purpose of creating a new talent experience within your organization, it is important to ask yourself what your own personal charter around change is. What is your own personal charter around the experience you would like to see within the organization? What are the underlying principles you want to connect to for the future state of the organization?

There is no right answer to this question, no one-size-fits-all charter! Everyone will answer this question differently. Everyone will create a different charter that is true to their own vision for their own organization. This is a really important starting point for effecting true, lasting change.

Creating a charter is a process of reflection. And it's not one you have to do without help. Within the Fuel50 platform is a tool that helps you craft a vision statement and a purpose statement. If you'd like some assistance and guidance in creating your charter, please access our tool via this link on our website: www.fuel50.com/VisionCreatorrequest

You can help deliver change to your organization just by starting to live your values and championing them so consistently that others remember you for it.

We have recently witnessed revolutionary change happen at grassroots level with the #MeToo and Black Lives Matter movements. People have become impatient for change, and we can no longer stand still and tolerate outdated practices.

"We need to be brave and take chances on growth and opportunity," Larry McAlister, vice president of global talent at NetApp, said in response to our survey on talent mobility and the future of work. "We can't assume there is a perfect candidate in the external marketplace when we already have someone ready to make a career leap internally; we need to have faith in the capabilities, agility, and resilience of our people to help us leap into the future. Diversity, inclusivity, and belongingness must be viewed as a business transformation task and not a project. It must be baked into everything we do, from the board to the employee experience to our internal and external brand. The democratic, employee-first and inclusive principles of a talent marketplace are helping us execute on this transformation plan."

Organizations who are fair, transparent, inclusive, and respectful of their people are the ones who will thrive into the future. We need a more human and humane work experience, and the time to make that change is here. Talent practices will be better than they were last decade: more human, more people centric, more intelligent, more robust in their skills and capability matching, more learning- and growth-oriented, more enabling, and better able to deliver the talent optimization that organizations will need in the coming decade.

All of this is possible with the democratizing power of a talent marketplace, like the one we offer on our Fuel50 platform. As Josh Bersin writes,

> I've interviewed more than 50 companies using these systems and it's clear to me that [the Talent Marketplace] is one of the most successful innovations in HR. Every company that adopts this kind of solution sees almost immediate positive results, and over time this platform becomes one of the most popular systems in the company.... While I can't predict where this will go, I've now come to the conclusion that the Talent Marketplace market ... is becoming a new center for HR Tech. As these systems grow in maturity and purpose, companies are going to use them for more every day.[135]

The time is now. The new era of talent experience and talent enablement is here. We have been waiting for this moment. Together, we can create a utopian world where everyone across the globe has fair, equitable access to opportunities for their future, to the betterment of all.

Will you join us in the talent revolution?

---

135 Josh Bersin, "The Mad Scramble to Lead the Talent Marketplace Market," Josh Bersin, December 13, 2021, https://joshbersin.com/2021/12/the-mad-scramble-to-lead-the-talent-marketplace-market/.